Food Drying at Home

By
Bee Beyer

Published by J. P. Tarcher, Inc.

Los Angeles

Distributed by St. Martin's Press
New York

Dedication

To my parents, whose loving virtues taught me to love and serve God, people, and country; to want to work to the best of my abilities to achieve a higher level of thinking and living for all—and to those who in their own fields are also contributing toward a better life for everyone.

Library of Congress Catalog Card Number: 75-38009

Distributor's ISBN 312-90546-7
Publisher's ISBN 0-87477-049-1

Manufactured in the United States of America
Designed and illustrated by The Committee

Published by J. P. Tarcher, Inc.
9110 Sunset Blvd., Los Angeles, Calif. 90069

Published simultaneously in Canada by Macmillan of Canada
70 Bond St., Toronto, Canada M5B IX3

3   4   5   6   7   8   9   0

Acknowledgments: Many people have been extremely helpful in providing knowledge, material, time, and effort to make this book possible. I am indebted to Dr. Philip J. Welsh, Dr. John Douglas, Bea Palmer, Jan Hillus, Frances Paulson, Reba Staggs, as well as to many of my students who supplied material to make my writing task easier. Even my two little girls, Lisa and Gemma, cooperated by performing extra duties so that mother could write. Special thanks to my publisher, Jeremy P. Tarcher, for his special interest in the book; and to Lucy Barajikian, Pat Keeney, and Brian Williams for their editorial help.

Table of Contents

Introduction

During eight years on television as hostess of a syndicated cooking and consumer education show, I interviewed many outstanding, dedicated doctors and nutritionists whose goals were to encourage the growing and purchasing of organically raised food and to present it in its most nutritious form. The results of their research—which approached the subject from many different angles and points of view—convinced me that eating foods prepared without undue processing, preservatives or additives (including salt, sugar, and white flour) was the royal road to good health.

On my own, as a food consultant interested in helping people, I worked to develop a natural—preservative and additive-free—method for drying foods at a low temperature to best preserve both flavor and nutrition that would be next best to fresh. Over the years my own diet changed from rich sauces and fancy dishes—the very kinds of food I used to test and photograph for large food companies—to a simpler and unquestionably healthier diet. And as my diet changed, my vitality and enjoyment for life grew. I found myself facing each day simply feeling better. What happened to me can happen to you. Through this book, I want to share my experiences as a food consultant and teacher and bring to you the health, enjoyment, and even significant financial savings I have found in food drying—the natural way.

—Bee Beyer

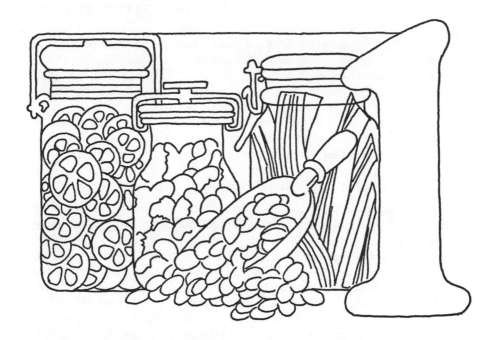

The Promises of Food Drying

Why should I dehydrate food? This is what I used to ask myself when I came across dried foods while working as a food writer and food consultant, and doing my own television cooking programs. Because dehydrated foods never looked especially appetizing, I often passed them by. Eventually, however, I decided to look into this old, yet new, way of preserving. After all, taste is the test, not appearance.

I acquired a simple dehydrator and began experimenting at home. I started with tomato, and to my amazement, the first time I put one of my dried tomato slices in my mouth, I experienced a flavor I'd never known before. Contrary to all expectations, it didn't taste "dry" at all, but fresh. Moreover, it had much more of a concentrated flavor than even a fresh tomato. Why? Because dehydration is a process in which moisture is removed, and so the natural flavor is enhanced.

Next I tried a banana slice. It, too, was terrific, delightfully chewy, filled with its own natural sweetness. In fact, it was almost like candy, although no sugar or honey had been added. One slice led to two, then to three, and then to twenty, and I found myself eating banana slices like peanuts.

Zucchini chips were the most refreshing surprise of all. Not only did drying enhance their natural flavor, but it made them taste as if salt had been added, although none had. Later, I found out that this is because vegetables contain a certain amount of natural salt, and when moisture is removed, this salty taste too is intensified.

In my work as a home economics teacher, I had always thought that fresh food was the only way to tantalize the palate as well as supply the best nutrition, but this episode opened up a whole new, exciting world for me. My main purpose in writing this book, then, is to share my experiences and natural food drying methods with you.

Actually, you are already familiar with many dried foods. Consider how many you buy and use each day: pasta, such as spaghetti, macaroni, noodles; beans, such as lentils, lima beans, navy beans, white beans, butter beans, soybeans, dried peas; spices, such as cinnamon, pepper, oregano, mustard seed, cardamon, basil, rosemary, onion flakes, garlic powder, parsley; grains and seeds, such as rice, wheat, oats, corn, barley, millet, rye, sesame seeds, sunflower seeds; coffee, cocoa, tea, nuts, soups, one-dish meals, cereals, cake mixes, and cookie mixes, potatoes, milk, eggs, cheeses. Even dog and cat food is available in dehydrated form.

I wanted to match this terrific variety by drying at home without having to add harmful additives, so I began teaching classes and experimenting with all kinds of dehydrators, from the crudest homemade to the most refined factory models. After I had been teaching a while, manufacturers approached me to test their equipment. Some of the best ones I sold or recommended to others, and have since developed two models of my own.

All of this was quite a change from my experiences as a child growing up in rural Kansas, where we used not-too-satisfactory sun-drying methods for apples, beans, apricots, and the like. Indoor home dehydrators completely captivated me, and I gradually developed a natural method of drying that does not require additives or preservatives. Although fresh food is the best form of diet, and I am not trying to encourage the substitution of dried foods for fresh, still dehydrated is superior to canned or frozen food. Thus this book shows you how to dry foods yourself at home without destroying nutrients by high temperature or added preservatives. Food drying is as old as time, but the procedures I use simplify the whole operation so that you can become masters of the art with hassle-free ease, the natural way.

But to return to the opening question: why dry food? I will go into the details of economics, ease of use, storage, and the like later, but here let me just show what you may have been missing.

IT'S DELICIOUS!

Call it what you will, flavor or taste, when serving food, this must be of primary consideration. If it doesn't *taste* good, if it's not delicious, no one is going to be interested in eating what you dry, no matter how good it looks or how nutritious it may be. But the joy of dried foods lies in the fact that, believe it or not, it is *more* flavorful than fresh. For instance, fruit, when it is dried, is infinitely sweeter, almost like candy. Once you make your own raisins, you'll never want to buy the commercially prepared ones again—and the same can be said for just about every product you learn to prepare in this book.

IT'S EASY TO PREPARE

The process is so simple to prepare it's hard to believe. Here are the five basic steps to drying food:

1. Wash the food, and eliminate anything spoiled. Use only what is in peak condition—perfect for eating.

2. Slice, dice, chop, chunk, shred. (Nothing is wasted. You put the ends and odd pieces of fruit into a blender to puree for "leather," as we'll describe.)

3. Place the sliced, diced, or chopped food directly on trays.

4. Put the trays into the dehydrator for the required drying time, which can vary from 2½ hours (for crackers, teas, herbs, sliced mushrooms) to 40 hours (for juicy plum halves). I often let the dehydrator do the work while I'm sleeping

5. When dry, remove the food from the trays and store in airtight containers in a cool, dry, dark place.

That's how easy it is to prepare. There's no mystery about it

IT'S EASY TO USE

Since dehydration is a matter of removing the moisture, all you need to do when you're ready to use the dried product is put the moisture back. You can do this in three ways:

1. **Eat the dried food as is, in its dried state.** It will reconstitute naturally on your tongue. This may also be the best way. In fact, in my family we're perfectly content to eat as much as 80 percent of our dehydrated food without any reconstituting at all. Once, for instance, right in the middle of the fresh peach season, my little girl Gemma, age 10, sat eating a handful of dried peach slices just out of the dehydrator. Next to her was a bucket of fresh, juicy, sweet peaches

waiting to be eaten. I tried to explain to her that it would be better to eat the fresh peaches now while they were still available and store the dried ones for later enjoyment—to which she replied, "But the dry ones taste better!" What could I say? She was right. After school my other daughter, Lisa 12, often eats just-dried tomato slices right off dehydrator trays, although the refrigerator may be full of ripe tomatoes ready for slicing. Thus, don't be surprised if you and your family find yourselves eating a high percentage without reconstituting.

2. Add water to the dried food. In a short time, the food will be ready to eat, taste-fresh as it was originally. Or you may wish to add it to a number of other ingredients to make one of the delicious recipes I describe later.

3. Powder the dried food. Puree it with liquid in a blender for use in soups, sauces, yogurt, ice cream, cakes, breads, and many other dishes. This process is also covered in detail later.

IT SAVES YOU MONEY

Food drying is a fantastic way to save. For example, in one year alone, I saved over $370 by dehydrating my own tomatoes for juice, catsup, sauce, slices, paste, and soup (and this was just for tomatoes!). My children love all kinds of fruit "leathers," (pureed fruit dried in a sheet) but the ones I prepare cost only 8¢ a roll, rather than up to 79¢ commercially.

The electricity needed to operate a home dehydrator costs not much more than a penny an hour—imagine, 60 minutes of use for only 1¢! In fact, the low temperature maintained in the dehydrator makes its operating costs less expensive than those for other appliances.

IT'S HEALTHIER

Good flavor, convenience, and economy notwithstanding, no one should have to eat "empty" food. A U.S. Department of Agriculture chart (see Appendix) shows that dehydrated food is more nutritious than canned or frozen. The reason is that cooking or canning at high temperature destroys about 65 percent of the original food value. Thus, according to the Institute of Food Technologists, canned or cooked food retains only about 35 percent of its original vitamin C content. One reason for the superb nutritional value of dried food, then, is that you haven't cooked the food literally to death. You can prove this to yourself. If you take seeds from tomato slices dried in the way I recommend and plant them, they will germinate, sprout, and grow. Even dried, therefore, nutrition and life still remain in a tomato slice

IT'S EASY TO STORE

Dehydrated food is extremely compact and requires very little space as compared to frozen or canned. The ratio in size of fresh to dried food ranges from 4 to 1 to as much as 25 to 1, depending on the moisture content of the food and how much you dry it. It is a great advantage to be able to store a convenient supply on one kitchen shelf (or even under your bed). For example, 20 pounds of tomatoes would when canned fill 11 quart jars but when dried weigh 1 pound, 2 ounces, and fill one #10 can. Five pounds of mushrooms (or of green peppers) would dehydrate to 1 pound; 4 pounds of beef would make 1 pound of beef jerky; 4 pounds of fresh bananas would dry to 1 pound, 4 ounces; 4 pounds of fresh apples would dry to 1 pound.

IT PROVIDES CONVENIENCE AND VARIETY

Have you ever had a hankering for strawberries when they weren't in season? Or for mushrooms when they were too expensive? Or for butterfish when the market was too far away? Turn your disappointments into drying, for if you dry these foods when available in season, at prices you can afford, and pack and store them on your shelves, they'll be ready to use when you want them. Entire meals can be packed in little bags and carried along in pocket, purse, or suitcase. When I take a tiny packet out of my purse for lunch, my companions sometimes look at it curiously—"Is that all you're going to eat?"—until they find out that small amount is pure food, containing a good deal more nutrition than the usual lunch of a white-bread sandwich, potato chips, and soft drink.

Later I have more information on the convenience of dried foods for brown baggers, travelers, and backpackers.

IT'S GREAT FOR ANY EMERGENCY

As I look around me at the jars and bags of food delicacies of all varieties, colors, shapes, and taste, it gives me a good feeling to know that I am prepared for almost anything—whether a natural disaster or just an interruption in normal shopping and cooking—and that I can whip up a delicious meal in seconds from the dried food larder. I always have on hand a good supply of beef jerky and dried fish, a variety of vegetables and fruits, grains, fruit leathers, noodles, yeast, and herbs.

SOME QUICK ANSWERS

The benefits seem endless, and so are the questions my students ask. Here are some answers I've given to questions you may never have thought about.

Yes, everything (almost) can be dehydrated. The "almost" is fat, which turns rancid, though the book tells you later how to deal with this when dehydrating meat. Artichoke hearts can be dehydrated, but I'm not at all sure you'd find the leaves worth the time and effort. (But you probably never thought of dehydrating artichokes anyway.)

Yes, dried food has the same calories as fresh. Rest assured, there is no way that a dried apricot half or any other dried product can contain *more* of anything than the original fresh one did, simply *because nothing is added*—no sugar, no salt, no syrup, no flour. The nutrients are now concentrated in a smaller area, but there is little change in the caloric content. Some of the action that occurs in toasting bread also occurs in the drying process. Fresh bread is quite heavy in starch. When you toast it, some of that starch changes to a natural sugar, making it easier to digest and lowering calories slightly.

Yes, children adore dried foods. Parents sometimes wonder whether their children will eat dehydrated food. Let me just say that when I was in the process of testing recipes for this book, my children came in from school and cleared off half a tray of turkey jerky, strawberry slices, ground beef, and taco mix, before I could open my mouth to say, "How was your day?" If you have a problem, it will be the reverse—trying to keep dried food around long enough to pack and store and put away.

No, you don't have to buy bushels of food to dry. For one thing, you can dry a whole assortment of foods all at one time. There is no need to load your dehydrator to capacity. Even a tray or two with a combination of food will dry beautifully. In addition, you can put your dryer to use to make such superb concoctions as yogurt, crackers, cookies, cottage and cream cheese, noodles, granola, tea.

No, it won't be like some kitchen equipment which you use only twice a year. If you buy a compact, portable dehydrator and keep it on the counter in your kitchen, you can use it all year round, taking full advantage of the specials at the market and drying as often as you wish.

No, you don't have to preblanch, soak, sulphur, or add anything to your food. The old-fashioned methods of sun drying and oven drying were often heavily dependent on chemicals and preservatives. The techniques used in the natural way of food drying do not require them. You do not want to take away any nutrients by preblanching or soaking, nor use any harmful additives or chemicals, and when drying naturally, there is no need to.

No, it doesn't take much of your time. The natural system eliminates all of the preprocessing steps. Once in the dryer, the trays do not need to be rotated or the food rearranged. (Some people do like to turn slices over to dry them faster, but it is not necessary.)

Yes, you can dry food in the sun or oven, but there are problems.
A home food dryer is easier and produces a more superior product
with less problems. (We'll go into this in detail later.)

Yes, there is a definite aesthetic quality about dried products. Wait
till you see the rosy-hued, strawberry-rhubarb leather; the delicate,
green-rimmed cucumber ring; the sand-dollar look of a crispy banana chip. All have a beauty of their own, and will woo the eye in
this new vision of the food world. Unfortunately, we have so long associated the words *wrinkled* and *shriveled* with age that we may need to
coin a few new ones to describe the way foods look after drying because
the adjectives now just don't fit the picture. Since only the freshest
and choicest of food is selected to dry, it is food at its best. That peak
fresh flavor is captured and kept right up to the moment you pop it
into your mouth.

Yes, even a single person can benefit from a home dryer. You don't
have to have a large family to make it worthwhile, or live on a farm,
or have a vegetable garden to consider this method of preserving. Nor
does it have geographical limitations. And single people can benefit
because they are on the run and do not like to spend a lot of time
cooking.

Dried food does not sound tempting. Tempt me. Let me try. How does
this sampling sound to you? They're all in this book and can be prepared in a dehydrator or made with products you have already dried:
Fruit Cream Cheese Pinwheels, Sweet Sour Spareribs, Orange Delight Cake, Pineapple Banana Leather, Heavenly Fruit Bars, Meal in
a Snack, Granola, Beef and Turkey Jerky, Strawberry Jam.

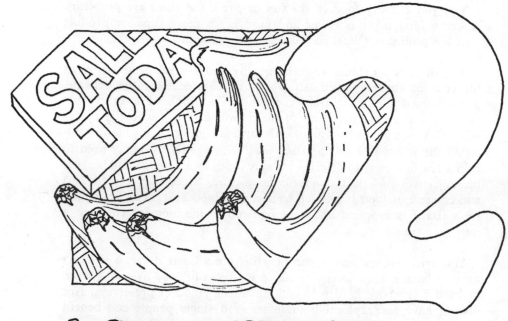

A Super Way to Save-- in a Big Way

Just as zucchini slices when dried shrink right down to the size of a thin dime, so do food costs when drying food the natural way. The amount you save by dehydration can be considerable, for if you buy wisely and use a well-designed dehydrator, you can save 50 to 60 percent of your fresh food-buying dollars. And the initial cost of your investment in a dehydrator is not only returned within a short time, but it will continue to help you save in numerous ways all through your lifetime. The percentage can go even higher if you have your own fruit and vegetable garden.

Here are seven ways you can save:

—by buying and drying in season,
—by looking out for grocery specials,
—by generating your own specials,
—by the ultimate special, getting produce free,
—by using *all* your garden produce,
—by sharing other people's gardens,
—by wasting nothing in your own kitchen.

Let me quickly describe each of these.

SEASONAL SAVINGS

Food costs are lower when food is most abundant, so buy food in season. Buy enough to eat fresh, then dry and store a supply for those months when the product is scarce and prices are high. This way you can eat whatever you want throughout the whole year without spending an exorbitant amount.

For those who like to calculate, let me give you one example. For myself and my two girls I dry 400 pounds of fresh tomatoes each year. Four hundred pounds? Did your jaw drop? Well, hang onto the book so I can explain that I dry a lot more than the average family because of my deep involvement in the food-drying field. Let me also add that I dry my tomatoes into slices. I then powder some and, depending on the amount of water added, reconstitute the powder into paste, sauce, catsup, soup, and juice. So you can see that this quantity of 400 pounds encompasses a great many by-products that you might not ordinarily figure into your tomato needs.

Now, of course, I want to get the best buy for my money, so I buy in season. This is how I worked it one year. In June tomatoes in my area were almost $1 a pound. I waited until September when tomatoes were in abundance, then purchased 20 lugs—a lug weighs 20 pounds—in an outlying area where they cost only $1.50 per lug. The total cost came to $30—not the $400 I would have paid if I had bought them out of season. So right there, I saved $370. But by waiting until September, even if I had purchased tomatoes in town at 39¢ a pound, I would still have saved a total of $244. Of course, if you are a one- or two-member household or hate catsup or spaghetti, your tomato needs might be a lot less. (And, naturally, if tomatoes give you a rash, you won't be drying any at all.) But take any other fruit or vegetable, buy in season in quantity, and dry for days when prices escalate. It's one smart way to economize.

GROCERY SPECIALS

Stores have sales all the time—anniversary sales, expansion sales, closing out specials, special specials. Keep your eyes peeled for them. Buy as much as you need to eat fresh, and then buy a bit more to dry. Put the extras in the dehydrator along with whatever other items you happen to have around. Dry. Then store.

In my neighborhood beef jerky sometimes sells locally for 49¢ a half ounce, or $16 a pound. It's the kind of item that disappears like magic at my house, since it is extremely convenient for snacks, for carry-along meals, or for brown baggers who pack it along with dried tomato, banana, and apple slices. By watching the specials, I can purchase lean round steak for $1.27 a pound. If I purchase four pounds for $5.08, this will yield approximately 1 pound of finished beef jerky—making a whopping savings of $11 per pound.

MAKE YOUR OWN SPECIALS

Don't just sit around waiting for the specials to appear. Go to your local market and make your grocer an offer he can't refuse. You will find him very receptive, for the produce department of large chain markets or grocery stores usually has "pulls" every day. "Pulls" are the delicious, fully ripe, not-yet-beginning-to-spoil fruits and vegetables that are removed daily from the rest of the produce display. They are delicious and fully edible since they are quite ripe. However, they bruise easily and need to be used immediately, so they are often sold at very low prices.

Let me give you one example of what can be done so that every bit of what you buy is used and nothing is wasted. Go to the market and look for fully ripe bananas that are speckled, quite brown, but still fairly firm. These bananas have had more time for the flavor and nutrition to develop and are tastier than the firm, yellow-green ones. Besides, they are cheaper. On all counts, they are perfect for dehydrating. Offer the store manager about 5¢ or 6¢ a pound for them. (Occasionally, he may even give them to you free.) And then do what I do.

I have walked out of my neighborhood store with a Number 10 bag-load of bananas for which I have paid 60¢ instead of the $2.60 it would have cost to purchase the yellow-green ones at 26¢ a pound. Since they will not keep long, I have to dehydrate them immediately. I place two dehydrator trays side by side: one for chewy or crisp banana chips, the other for banana fruit roll or leather. Thus, you can reduce expenses each month by buying and drying a variety of advertised specials, or generating your own at local markets.

THE ULTIMATE SPECIAL—FREE

Sometimes produce is given away free to needy individuals or groups. With a dehydrator it is then a simple matter to dry and store, and if done on a regular basis, the economics of it will soon be evident.

Grocery stores are not the only source for free food. There are several areas of the country where people are permitted to go into agricultural fields to pick up what remains after the crops are harvested. (Often they are invited back year after year because after they leave the fields are cleared, ready for the next stage of farming.) College students have done this in the Midwest, older people ("senior gleaners") have done it in Northern California. By taking advantage of "gleaning," people can pick nutritious fresh fruits and vegetables, rather than leave them to rot, then dry the surplus. Obviously, a quality food dryer is an economic boon not only for individuals and families, but also for people in senior citizens homes, nursing homes, orphanages, and other charitable groups. People enjoy working together in the slicing, dicing, chopping. It is not difficult, yet it gives a feeling of accomplishment, and certainly pride when they see the beautiful stored food, which they can even give away as gifts in small baby food jars to relatives or friends—very welcome gifts of dried apple, banana, or tomato slices, as well as chopped green peppers, onion, or celery. (In fact, you might consider donating a dehydrator to one of these institutions as a helpful form of service.)

USING ALL YOUR GARDEN PRODUCE

In dead of winter, have you longed for the sun-ripened peaches your garden produced in summer—and that you had such trouble giving away because trees have a habit of producing all at once in such quantities that you would rather not even see another peach, let alone eat one? So many people are into gardening these days, and love it, except for this particular problem. The very thing they have worked so hard for—a good crop— becomes a problem as they look around for someone who hasn't already received a bagful.

What to do? Dry! The surplus harvest from gardens, fruit trees, and any other bumper crop can be dried for later use. You can enjoy peaches, and all your other garden-grown produce by slicing, dicing, leathering, and then drying to enjoy them at intervals all year round, instead of nonstop eating for six golden weeks. There is no better way to prolong the season.

Herbs also can be grown by anyone. Even those who have only one windowsill can have a pot or two. Enjoy herbs when fresh and green. Dry what you can't use for later use. You have probably paid, and paid dearly, for the varieties available at the markets. Now enjoy them for almost no outlay of money.

SHARING GARDENS

If you don't have a yard or a garden, or even a container garden on patio or porch, you can still help the elderly or handicapped pick their fruit trees, share the joys of nature, and be a good neighbor all at the same time.

The son of a friend of mine is blind and cannot pick the golden, juicy apricots in his backyard. His mother asked if I knew anyone who might help. I volunteered myself and two daughters, and in two sessions we harvested 160 pounds (not including the fruit that went immediately into our stomachs). We dehydrated some into apricot leather and the rest into apricot halves, gave half to the owner, and reserved the rest (per her request) for our own enjoyment. Our golden treasure was all free, except for a little labor and the small amount of energy it cost to dry. We also had the great pleasure of helping a disabled friend.

Next, we found a lovely little lady who had plum, fig, and nectarine trees. She was too elderly to climb any ladders, so once again, Lisa, Gemma, and I volunteered to harvest the crop, and followed the same procedure. Now we also have a nice supply of home-grown, home-dried prunes, figs, and nectarines, free of charge.

There are other kinds of harvests, too. When friends or relatives go fishing, we are blessed with many pounds of fish. Again, what we can't eat, we dry.

WASTING NOTHING IN YOUR KITCHEN

Who hasn't had food left over after a party or a holiday dinner and spent days eating it over and over in an attempt to finish it before it spoiled?

This happened once when I served Teriyaki Steaks and Sukiyaki to some dinner guests. A lot of thin meat slices and vegetables were left (carrots, celery, onion, green pepper, tomato), cut but still un-cooked. I put them all into the dehydrator, flipped on the switch, and went to bed. When I woke up the next morning, everything was properly dried, enabling us to enjoy all that good food at our leisure. Special dinner parties or holidays are also great occasions to trans-form leftover turkey or chicken into turkey and chicken rolls.

Refrigerators get overstocked at other times as well, and again a dehydrator can come to the rescue. It's the very thing to use, even for a small amount of food. You need not load it to capacity every time you use it. Even a trayful can be prepared. Cost is minimal and drying effective, whether trays are all full or not.

Taking advantage of any or all of these seven ways should help reconstitute your shrinking food dollars in a hurry.

The Natural Way to Dry

The difference between natural food drying and what I would call unnatural food drying is that in the first method there is no preblanching and no adding of chemical preservatives or additives.

NO PREBLANCHING

Blanching, the placing of food into hot water, was done in older methods of preserving in order to kill the enzymes that cause the organic changes in food. You do not want to kill food value. All you want to do is render the activity dormant. As with almost everything else in this world there are two schools of thought here, but all I know is what practical experience has taught me. To the hundreds of other people who dry food, as well as the hundreds more I have taught, blanching is not necessary. Food will keep beautifully with color, flavor, and nutrients intact for extended periods of time if you follow the instructions in this book. Blanching destroys food value. In the case of corn, it turns good nutrition to starch. It destroys fresh flavor because you are providing a hot bath that will make the food taste "cooked," not fresh and in the long run it will cost you time and money eating up all those kettles of water.

NO CHEMICALS, PRESERVATIVES, ADDITIVES

In my food-drying method I use no chemicals at all. I feel it is not only unnecessary, it is unhealthy. The freshest of foods will come out the choicest of dehydrated products drying the natural way because no chemicals, preservatives, additives, no sugar, salt, or flour are introduced, not even sulphur.

Sulphur was used originally to prevent sun-dried fruit from discoloring. According to government reports, discoloring does not affect food value and you pay premium prices in health food stores for unsulphured, sun-dried apricots that have turned completely black. If properly dried in a home food dehydrator, apricots need not turn black, as I'll explain later, and maybe they'll do for you what they have done for the Hunza.

The Hunza are a group of people living in an isolated area of the northwest frontier of Kashmir who eat many fresh apricots as well as those dried on the roofs of their homes. They have no preservatives, sprays, insecticides, pesticides, nor do they eat any sugar, salt, or refined flour. They begin and end each day with prayer, get lots of exercise and fresh air, and drink water rich in natural minerals. Their male members are reported to live to be 140 to 150 years of age, play and work vigorously, and still produce children at that advanced age. This may not be exactly the result you want from your dried food diet, but it sure is not a bad goal!

In our country today, newspaper and magazine headlines are proclaiming the possible link between cancer, birth defects, and other diseases because of the chemicals put into, and onto, our soil, plants, animals, and processed foods. This fact alone should encourage all of us to avoid the consumption of the chemical-laden items on our dining tables. *Forbes* magazine (March 15, 1976) reported that "the average person eats more than five pounds of chemical ingredients each year." A list of some of the chemicals you might be eating today is included in the appendix (courtesy Kay Rodgers of the Santa Monica Organic Garden and Nutrition Club). Sandwiches with luncheon meat and processed cheese can contain some of the numerous chemicals listed, all the way from mold inhibitor to plasticiser.

We eat so-called "enriched" flour. What does this mean? When wheat is processed, vitamin B complex and vitamin E are removed. (A shortage of these vitamins can cause problems with the heart, skin, eyes, nerves, digestion, and elimination.) Some attempt may be made by the processor to substitute artificial chemicals for the natural ingredients. Additional chemicals are pumped in as preservatives, so avoid products made from white flour. A lot of what we eat is treated this way.

In fact, let us go back one more step. Once the wheat kernel is broken, the food value of wheat deteriorates rapidly after three days according to many nutritional experts. Little can be said, therefore, for the prepared mixes, cereals, and flours that often take weeks to get to the stores and then sit on shelves till sold.

Although I am as busy as the next person, I still take the time to freshly grind grain each time I want to make bran muffins, quick breads, wafers, cereals, and noodles. Others I know who care about their family's health are also grinding their own every three days or so, making breads and cereals with no additives or preservatives. If you freeze the fresh-ground wheat flour or its products, it will keep nutrients longer than if you refrigerate or keep them at room temperature.

(Right eating might even have changed the course of history, for the Egyptian royal house in Biblical days ate breads made from white flour. The wheat germ and dark outer nutritious bran were left for the Hebrew slaves. In time, the slaves grew very strong. While it is not possible to lay the entire deterioration of the highly developed Egyptian civilization to their love for white flour products, I like to think it played a contributing role.)

Preservatives do not always have long names. Two common ones, sugar and salt, are added to most frozen and canned products today. When you dry food the natural way, *you do not add either sugar or salt*. This is important because authorities agree that they cause a number of physical problems.

About Preservatives

There are literally thousands of quotes available from nutritionists, doctors, and other authorities on the dangers to your health from highly processed food, preservatives, and additives put into much of the food that we eat every day. Among the leading offenders are sugar, salt, and flour.

". . . My research on coronary disease has convinced me beyond doubt that sugar plays a considerable part in this terrifying modern epidemic"—John Yudkin, M.D., *Sweet and Dangerous*

"Not only is the use of salt a cause of arthritis, it is also a factor in causing high blood pressure"—Dr. Philip J. Welsh, *How to Be Free from Arthritis Pain*

"Never eat any bread or bread products made with refined white flour. Twenty-seven of the natural nutrients have been milled out of it, including the vital [wheat] germ and the important vitamin B factors"—Paul G. Bragg, M.D., Ph.D., *Building Health and Youthfulness*

"The refining and/or processing of almost every food causes the loss of much or all of its nutritive value. White sugar, for example, retains not one milligram of vitamins or minerals. Furthermore, American markets are now flooded with synthetic or nearly synthetic 'foods' which contain little or no nutrients. All soft drinks, imitation 'fruit' ades, imitation fruit juices, gelatin desserts, and many other 'foods' are little more than sweetened chemicals. Besides harmful preservatives, a large percent of food contains so many additives, thousands are now used, that a correct label would look like the inventory of a chemistry supply room. Such additives may be harmless individually but combinations of them which no one has investigated could be highly toxic or even cancer producing"—Adelle Davis, *Let's Eat Right to Keep Fit*

"Everywhere, throughout the land, people are actually committing nutritional suicide by eating chemically treated devitalized food—the silent killer"—John Cullen, *Stop Killing Yourself and Begin to Live*

Doctors report that metabolism is affected when salt enters the system and recommend low sodium and salt-free diets in cases of arthritis, high blood pressure, obesity, epilepsy, dropsy, migraine, and nervous tension. The food industry continually adds salt and other preservatives to many convenience foods. When it is added to baby food, doctors believe it can cause arthritis or high blood pressure when the child reaches adulthood.

If you dry food the natural way, there is no need to soak apples, apricots, and potatoes in salt water or acid solution to prevent discoloration. Also vegetables already contain some natural salt and will taste salted once moisture is removed. Reduce the intake of salt in the rest of your cooking by substituting herbs such as oregano, rosemary, as well as garlic, onions, and other natural seasonings, or use the salt substitute I discuss later, which is made of ground dehydrated seaweed, tomato powder, and mustard seed.

Refined sugar is called "the quiet killer," robbing the system of calcium and contributing toward the incidence of heart disease, diabetes, and ulcers. Processed foods are loaded with it. When you dry food the natural way, honey (not sugar) can be used as a natural sweetener. The honey in metal containers is the kind you should buy since this is usually honey sold in its natural state. Normally, it does not have a clear quality so that is why distributors use metal. Honey in glass jars often has been processed, with sugar water added to beautify it.

At this point it will not come entirely as a surprise to the reader to discover that I am something of a fanatic about nutrition. So let me move away for a moment from the benefits of food drying without preservatives or additives to share with you a few facts and ideas that are important to me.

From the time children are fed their first jars of baby food, a wide variety of what are proving to be unhealthy additives are automatically included in their diet. For instance, in the October 2, 1975 *Los Angeles Times* it was reported that a leading brand of pudding for babies derived 27 to 44 percent of its calories from the addition of sugar, and it was only added by the manufacturers to please mothers. Authorities believe that this diet so early in a child's life can increase the tendency to obesity, create a "sweet tooth" habit, and increase cavities in later life.

School lunches are not much better because they are made from refined and canned foods, high in sugar. Besides, it has distressed many parents to see the candy, sweet drinks, and empty calorie foods their children consume from school vending machines. You'll be happy to know there are some moves toward improving the nutritional standards in schools. School boards are being encouraged to replace the

empty foods with fresh fruit and fruit and vegetable juices, because the snacks lack nutrition and may affect children's classroom behavior. Some school boards have already initiated such changes.

For your babies as well as your older children, food drying can help you provide them with healthier foods. Mothers can easily and inexpensively made baby food themselves. Puree fruits, vegetables, or meats in a blender. Dry any leftover into leather or fruit roll. When you wish to use it, tear in pieces, put back in the blender with a little water or juice. Older babies enjoy chewing dried fruit, as it is—it will reconstitute in their mouths! If your children do not already carry their lunches from home, you might consider fresh and dehydrated fruits and vegetables, beef and turkey jerky, nuts, seeds, and foods made from fresh ground whole grains.

Perhaps it is also time to begin reading the ingredients listed on some of our most popular boxed cereals. You will see that the ingredients are listed in order of quantity used. The major one is often sugar. That means there is more sugar than grain in what you buy—and eat. You might get more food value if you threw the contents away and ate the box. Since manufacturers produce what customers buy, if we stop buying this counterfeit food and demand quality, it will contribute toward upgrading the products now on our market shelves.

End of speech. Now back to food drying.

Food drying is probably as old as agriculture itself. Farmers have always used the sun to dry and cure hay, seeds, and grain. For centuries, the Japanese have prepared dried fish and jerky. Vikings and others who spent long periods at sea took along dried apples, meat, and assorted vegetables on their voyages. The American Indians used to cut meat in thin strips and hung them from trees to dry in the sun, and the early settlers hung green beans above the fire and primitive stoves to dry for use during severe winter months. All these people knew that the process worked, but they didn't know why.

Why does dried food keep? Because when moisture is carried off, bacteria—which is classified as a tiny plant and which causes food to spoil— cannot grow. Proper drying is the key to eliminating this problem, so I want to underscore the need to dry at the right temperature and for the right amount of time.

LOW TEMPERATURE SUPERIOR TO HIGH

Again, there are two schools of thought on the best temperature at which to dry. My experience based on years of experimentation and drying with all different recommended procedures and temperatures is that *drying at low temperatures—between 110 and 118 degrees—is* vastly superior on almost every count (color, flavor, nutrition) to high temperatures.

Let's look at the differences.

Nutrients

Low Temperatures. One of the main reasons for drying is that you want to preserve natural nutrients. Low temperatures sustain life. Humans can live at this temperature, and so does the life in a seed, as you discovered in the first chapter. Your goal is to create a dormant —not dead—state. Demonstrate this for yourself in another way. This time take yeast dough. Spread it on plastic wrap or parchment paper. Dry it at the low temperature. Then reconstitute it and use to make yourself some pizza or fresh-baked loaves of bread. The yeast will multiply and increase. The life and nutrients have not been destroyed.

High Temperatures. High temperatures destroy food values. As I pointed out earlier, fruits and vegetables exposed to high temperatures are deprived of approximately 65% of their nutritional value.

Quality of Product

Low Temperatures. Low temperatures retain "fresh" flavor and color. People in my classes always have the opportunity to taste food that has been properly dried at this low temperature, and they are astonished at the totally marvelous flavor, almost like fresh, that is maintained, and the retention of the natural color of fruits and vegetables.

High Temperatures. High temperatures can burn, carmelize, or scorch your food, especially if you use heat that is up to 140 degrees or over, changing not only the flavor, but color and nutrition as well.

Time and Attention

Low Temperatures. Low temperatures enable you to dry a variety of food at the same time without constant attendance. If you have put in an assortment of food of different thicknesses and qualities, different drying times will be required. With the low temperature it is not necessary to remember which trays to pull out at which time. All the food can be left in until the very last piece is dry—with no damage to the others dried earlier. I have left food in my own dehydrator for days when demonstrating at fairs and food-drying classes. The food did not overdry or burn. It did not lose flavor. It did not lose color.

Why should this be of interest to you? Let's bring this into the realm of practicality with this example. Say you put mushrooms and jerky and other foods which require only five hours to dry in the dehydrator at 9 P.M., a few hours before you go to bed. You do not care to wait up until 2 A.M. to take them out, nor do you want to set an alarm in order to wake up at 2. With this low heat, you can wait until the next morning to remove your dried food, the next evening, or even a day or two later, in the event that you are a trifle absent-minded or away on a trip. The product will be just as excellent.

When combining foods, there is just one precaution you should take. Do not mix a big quantity of strong-smelling or strong-tasting fish onion, garlic, or green pepper in with your other food since odor and flavor may be transferred. I say "big quantity" because I have dried half a tray of onions, green peppers, garlic, and fish, along with other fruits and vegetables, with no discernable exchange. The heat is so low that flavor and odors remain within the segments. However, if several trayfuls are put in and the fish happens to be a strong one, it is bound to make some difference in the other products drying at the same time.

High Temperatures. High temperatures demand constant attention. Trays need to be rotated and turned from front to back. You need to carefully watch to take trays out at exactly the "right" time to prevent scorching or burning.

HOW DRY IS DRY?

Specific information on whether a particular food is dry or not is given in the food sections. A little experience will quickly make you at least a semiexpert at knowing how dry is dry. But just to give you an indication at this point, you might be interested to know that properly dried food can be tested in a number of nonscientifically exact, but nevertheless kitchen-satisfactory, ways:

The Press Test. If you take a piece of dried food out of the dryer and press it, it will have a distinct characteristic. Strawberries and cranberries feel spongy. Apples are bendable and leathery. (They can also be dried crisper and break when bent.) Peas will powder when crushed in the blender. Onions break. Herbs crumble.

The Taste Test. Take a sample from the dryer. Taste it. It should be dry to the palate. It should not possess pockets or noticeable moisture in the center.

The Cut and Squeeze Test. Take a sample from the dryer. Cut it. There should be no moisture at the center. Take several pieces in your hand and squeeze together. No moisture should remain in your hand, and pieces should fall apart when released. Some fruit—such as figs, dates, cherries, raisins, and pears—will always be slightly sticky, even when properly dried, but they will still not stick together when stored.

The Weight Test. Twenty pounds of fresh tomatoes will dry to 1 pound, 2 ounces. That is one example of how much weight reduction there is in dried food. If you want a guide for yourself, compare the weight of your particular product by taking a pound of the fresh food and weigh it before you dry it. Then when it has dried enough, weigh it again. Or weigh a trayful when you are putting it into the dryer, then weigh again after it is dry. It will give you a basis to determine dryness the next time you prepare another batch.

DRYING TIMES

Drying times vary considerably due to a number of factors. Obviously, watermelon will take longer to dry than mushrooms and parsley because it is *juicier.* Even fruit from the same tree can vary because some are riper and *sweeter* than others, or they may be cut slightly *thicker,* or there is considerable *humidity* in the air when you are drying.

This brings to mind another story about one of my students who lives in a beach area. She was thrilled when she made her first banana slices in the evening hours after she got home from work. They were perfection. A few days later she decided to make another batch. It was a rather warm afternoon so she opened her windows wide and went to work. This time the chips did not get crisp. She had done everything exactly the same way, so she puzzled and thought and pondered and weighed the matter—until she happened to do some of her pondering looking out the window. Then it came to her. Her windows were wide open, letting in all that moist, humid, ocean air. The windows had been closed when she dried her first banana slices. It was just a matter of closing the kitchen window, putting the slices back in the dryer, and in no time she got what she was look ing for—perfectly crisp, light-colored banana chips.

To assure the best kind of drying, expose more surface. When food is thinly sliced or chopped, more surface of the food is exposed, making it easier for moisture to escape. That is why slicing food ⅛- to ¼-inch thick makes for quicker, more thorough drying. If food has been sliced too thick, a blister may appear on the outside because the outside dried first and pulled away from the center.

Of course in later chapters estimated drying times are provided for each fruit and vegetable. Here I just want to give you a preliminary idea: some herbs take 2½ hours; beef jerky, 5 hours; cucumbers, zucchini, corn, mushrooms, green peppers (sliced ⅛- to ¼-inch thick), 5 to 8 hours; peaches, apricots, apples (sliced ⅛- to ¼-inch thick), 8 to 9 hours; tomato slices (sliced ⅛- to ¼-inch thick), 12 to 14 hours; banana slices (sliced ⅛- to ¼-inch thick), 16 to 18 hours; large, sweet plum halves, 36 to 40 hours.

One of the nicest aspects of drying is that it is almost impossible to overdry at the 110 to 118 degrees that I recommend. So if in doubt, always dry for a little longer period of time.

NOTHING BETTER

Is there anything better than owning a quality home dehydrator, drying food the natural way, controlling what goes into what you eat, overseeing its entire processing? I think not. Your body deserves better treatment than what food processors are giving. Take care of it by growing your own food or purchasing that which is organically grown. Eat fresh and raw food. Or dehydrate it properly at a low temperature—the natural way—without sulphur, preservatives, or additives, and look forward to improved eating days ahead with a combination of fresh and dried foods on your family's bill of fare.

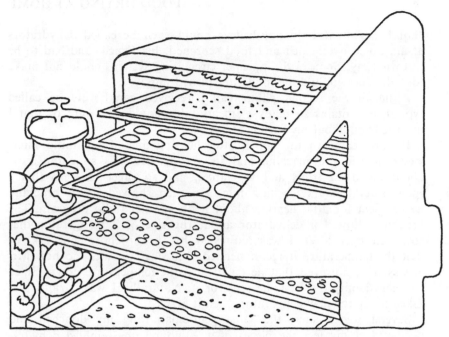

Happiness Is Owning a Home Food Dryer

The students in my classes share not only their food drying joys with me but their food drying woes as well. I have learned a lot from them, particularly in regard to the selection of a dehydrator, and I would like to pass on to you the pitfalls to avoid as well as the special features you should look for so that you will buy the best one available.

Perhaps the clearest way to demonstrate the extremes in experience is to tell you about two phone calls I received.

The first one came from a student who had been testing one of the food dryers I had suggested for several weeks. Even over the phone her voice carried great excitement. "It's wonderful!" she told me. "If all my furniture and entire household were repossessed, I think the only thing I'd care to hang on to would be my food dehydrator. It would be absolutely the last thing in my home I'd abandon." She immediately made plans to buy two more, one for each of her children.

Many of my other students have also been inspired to dry food, but in an attempt at economy they took less care in their choice of equipment and came back with tales of disappointment after experiencing every kind of food drying problem. Some had purchased "hot boxes" that I do not believe could even be called dehydrators at all. Some overheated and food scorched, blackened, and had to be thrown away. Some with improper circulating systems could not make food dry enough, and the food later turned moldy.

Although the second phone call I received can hardly be called typical, it contains so many elements you should be aware of that I must tell you about my friend, Mr. X.

He first came to my home, after hearing one of my radio interviews, to see the machine and its results. He was so enthusiastic about the dried fruits and vegetables, and so eager to learn that I spent several hours teaching him. He then showed me a brochure he had sent for after hearing about it on another radio program. The brochure showed a dehydrator about the size of a refrigerator that cost well over $200. I was impressed by the brochure, but I knew that the temperature it recommended, 140 degrees, was too hot. Mr. X was sure, however, that he could turn the temperature down. Since he wanted only the best, he sent for it. Naturally, I was curious and asked to see the new dehydrator when it arrived.

Several weeks later, the same gentleman rang my doorbell and deposited at my feet the pieces of a 90-pound unassembled dehydrator. If ever a man was disappointed, it was he, for not only was the dryer not of the same material as a refrigerator (it was of a weak-looking fiberboard), but the brochure had failed to mention that it would come unassembled, and from the looks of the numerous and complicated parts and instructions, it would take days to put together and he had Bing cherries waiting to be dried. I helped him dry his food, but he still had very much of an unresolved problem. He decided to take the unassembled pieces to his sister's home to assemble and leave with her for drying apricots. I heard nothing for a few days, and then came another phone call. It seems that his sister had attempted to dry apricot halves—only to have them burn and stick to the shelves. Since she couldn't separate them from the soft plastic shelves, Mr. X took them to the local car wash and blasted them off with water. The shelves had warped from the heat so he had to turn them upside down and weigh them with bricks in an attempt to straighten them.

I couldn't believe my ears; it would have made hilarious material for a filmmaker, except it should never have happened in real life.

The story should have ended there, but unfortunately it didn't. Mr. X followed my suggestion to write the company for new shelves and a new thermostat. They sent the shelves but charged him $10 for the thermostat and it still would not adjust to the proper temperature. This happened in June. My friend spent the rest of the summer tediously canning, having already spent close to $250 on not very

WRONG DEHYDRATOR

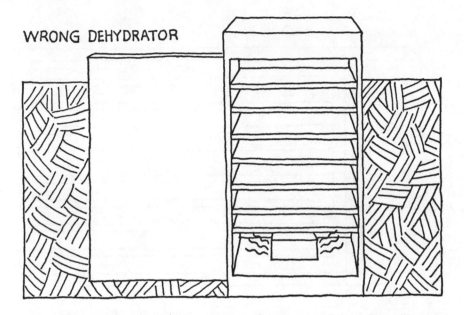

effective machinery and parts. The cherry-drying experience, how-ever, made him a staunch friend, for whenever he went to the country, he would bring back tree- and vine-ripened fruits and vegetables for himself and then share his abundance with me. In the doing, he had a chance to observe the lovely dried foods I prepared all summer. By August, he could stand it no longer (he had canned himself out of apartment space); and he finally bought a preassembled dehydra-tor that I recommended.

Now Mr. X was lucky; he had bought only one other dehydrator before he found one of good quality. Some have purchased three dehydrators before they found one that dehydrated foods properly. So to prevent a succession of tragic buying experiences and the sub-sequent waste of improperly dried food, here is a check list for you to follow when purchasing a home dehydrator to assure yourself of obtaining the best quality on the market.

FEATURES OF A GOOD DEHYDRATOR

Heating Element

Never purchase a dehydrator with the heating system on the bottom. The bottom shelves combined with a high temperature turn fruit dark and sticky, "cook" and not "dry" the food, and destroy valu-able nutrients. The uneven drying will also mean you have to keep

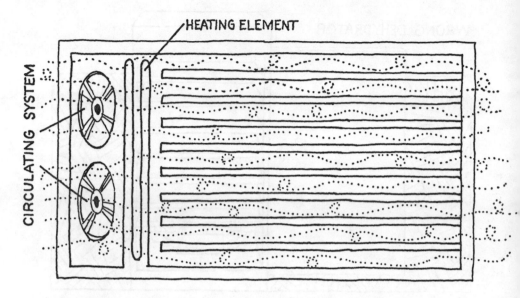

rotating the shelves, a needless time-consuming operation that keeps you in constant attendance during the drying process. One such contraption I tested with the heating element on the bottom also had no circulating "flow through" system or thermostat. The bottom shelf went up to 370 degrees, the center shelves to 250 degrees, and the top shelf to 150 degrees. Not at all desirable.

The heating element should be on the *back* or *side* of the dehydrator. This location enables the air to flow with uniform heat across all the trays so that the drying process is even from top to bottom. It means you can fill your dehydrator at night and go to sleep, resting assured that bottom trays will not overheat and overdry or scorch your food.

Thermostat

To maintain this desired constant, low temperature, you will want a dehydrator with a good thermostat. Avoid those that do not possess a thermostat; ones that come with an inferior one that cannot maintain constant, even heat; and especially those that are preset at too high a temperature. Buy the dehydrator that has either an adjustable thermostat (between 90 and 130 degrees) or one that is preset at the ideal temperature. For best results in drying, remember the internal temperature in a dehydrator should be about 110 to 118 degrees. Too low a temperature (such as 110 degrees and below) will make the satisfactory drying of many foods almost impossible. It will take such a long drying period (especially in moist or high humidity climates) that much of your food will spoil before it is properly dried.

Circulating System and Air Openings

If you lack a proper circulating system, drying at such low temperatures is even more difficult. The flow of warm air is what removes moisture from food. If the heating element and thermostat create the necessary uniform, warm, low temperature, a good circulating system, with definite air vents or openings, insures that air flows *into* the dryer and *out*. As fresh air comes in one opening, it should cross the shelves, pick up maximum moisture from the food, and carry it away from the drying foods through another vent and out of the dryer. If the same air is recycled across the food again, or over and over again, it is already saturated with moisture from the first trip and cannot pick up as much the second or third time across.

So for good air flow and distribution, a dehydrator will have openings (1) on the *left and right sides,* or (2) in the *front and back,* for the proper intake of fresh dry air and subsequent exhaust of moisture-laden air.

If your dryer just agitates the same air around at the low temperature, it makes it almost impossible to dry some foods adequately enough to prevent spoilage. The food may *appear* dry, indeed, the outside may *feel* dry, but in reality, there is still moisture inside, and it will spoil no matter how carefully you store it. Many of my students have attested to this, as they showed me dried food that had spoiled in storage because their dehydrator did not have a proper circulating system. Although it is true that a few food products can be dried successfully where the same air moves over the food again and again, others, such as tomatoes, figs, citrus fruit, leather usually cannot.

Tray Size

Now as to the matter of trays. Interestingly enough, size is important. One lady who attended one of my classes came up to me one day in church rather upset. "My stored dried food got moths in it, and I had to throw it all away." I began to question her to be sure she had dried it properly.

As the conversation developed, it became apparent that she had dried her food in a dehydrator her husband had built. The problem developed because he found some ordinary window screens measuring 30 by 30 inches (much too large) which he used for the trays with a lone center back circulating system. The tray areas were too wide for one central circulating system to cover properly. Thus the food on the sides and corners did not dry thoroughly. This left just enough moisture for the growth of existing life—in this case, moths!

Remember our food is grown in the great outdoors, and if sufficient moisture or water is not removed eggs or larvae (which may already be present in food from things flying in the air or existing in soil) will flourish even while the food is in storage. So food must be properly and adequately dried, and large trays just cannot do a good job unless there is a corresponding strong circulating system. A large tray size poses one other problem. It will sag in the middle unless made of extremely strong material because of the weight of the food, which is considerable on trays of that size.

Trays that have the best support to hold the weight of the food and dry it evenly and thoroughly are rectangular ones, about 11 by 15 inches or 15 by 17 inches. Each tray can hold about one or two pounds of food. They should not be too close together. About 1½ inches between shelves is adequate. If they are closer, make sure the dehydrator has a strong circulating system. The recommended number of trays in a unit is eight. If you have ten trays and they are too close together with an inadequate circulating system, it will not do as good a job of drying.

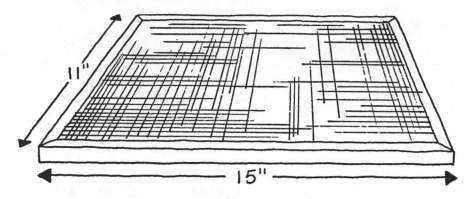

Tray Material

Remember that the food you eat goes directly onto the trays, so the material used is very important. Stainless steel mesh trays, although a trifle more costly, are best. Fiberglass trays are next best to stainless steel. Plastic shelves in a low temperature dehydrator could be safe but make sure they are nontoxic plastic.

Because of the uncertain health factors connected with plastic, I would be concerned about a dehydrator with plastic shelves if high heat was used, since leaching occurs at high temperatures.

Other metals, especially aluminum, should be avoided. Jethro Kloss in his book, *Back to Eden,* gives evidence of aluminum poisoning from food cooked in aluminum pots and pans. Therefore, I do not recommend that trays be made of aluminum mesh. (However, the edges of the trays can be held together by lightweight aluminum since food doesn't touch this portion.)

Avoid the type of tray that must be lined with cloth or nylon mesh when drying ordinary sliced fruits and vegetables. If you use my recommended low temperature, this is just a lot of unnecessary bother. If trays must be lined to prevent excessive sticking, the dehydrator is probably too hot. Trays, of course, must be lined for liquids or thin foods, such as soups, chilis, leathers, and stews, so that food will not run through.

I have very little problem whatever with food sticking to the trays. Tomatoes, pineapple, and bananas (which are juicier) "stick" slightly but are fairly easy to remove, once properly dry. I do not use any kind of spray or oil. Not only is it unnecessary, but any trace of oil left might turn rancid.

Do not choose mesh trays with large holes which must be lined to prevent beans, peas, cherries, and other small food particles from falling through.

Cabinet

I believe that a dehydrator for general use should be easy to clean and attractive enough to keep indoors. One of the best materials I have found is a lightweight copper or aluminum exterior which seems to maintain a more constant temperature throughout the cabinet. (Metal on the outside is permissible since there is no direct contact with food.) A formica-covered or heavy wood cabinet about ¾-inch thick also makes a good dryer. Dehydration is a natural process, and the natural materials seem to work very well but do avoid lightweight wood as it may warp after continuous use.

I have tested at least two other dehydrators that were metal with a baked-on enamel finish. For some reason, neither seemed to dry as well as the ones mentioned above.

Door

I prefer doors that open from one side to the other, rather than from top to bottom, only because the door is out of the way, to the side, making it more convenient to work with the shelves. Also, if not well made, in time they may flop open at odd moments. I also enjoy see-through acrylic doors because I like to see what's going on inside without opening to check.

MAINTENANCE

Trays. Trays are a simple matter to clean. Just place, standing up lengthwise, in your sink. Run hot water over them. Soak for a few minutes. Stuck dried food will reconstitute and can be easily sponged away in the hot water. Turn tray over. Sponge and wash. Rinse and dry.

Exterior. If the exterior is copper or aluminum, sponge with soapy water, then a clear-water wipe. If it is wood or formica, it is as easy to clean as a piece of furniture. Use a good furniture polish.

Interior. There is very little cleaning that needs to be done to the interior, since the low temperature prevents spatters or messy running juices. A simple soapy and clear-water sponging will clean up the few drops that may occur over a few months' time.

GUARANTEE

Any established reputable company will provide a guarantee with their product. Do not purchase any dehydrator without one. Moving parts should be guaranteed for six months to a year. Reputable companies stand behind their guarantee and make provisions for replacements. Electrical components should be U.L. (Underwriter Laboratory) approved.

THIS 'N THAT

1. A good quality dehydrator at this recommended temperature will never get hot enough to damage any walls, but leave about two inches of air space where air enters and leaves.

2. Several sizes are available. They can be as small as 12 inches by 13 inches by 24 inches. Buy the one that suits you and your family's needs. There are small compact, portable, counter models for individuals and small families, highly recommended because they can be kept in your kitchen for year-round use. Larger ones are available, too. But if it's handy, you will use it continuously. If it is attractive, it will look great in your kitchen. If it is compact, it will fit easily on a kitchen counter.

3. Make sure it has a quiet motor. You may be happy to know that food is drying, but you don't need to be constantly reminded.

OTHER HELPFUL EQUIPMENT

Here is a list of materials and equipment that will greatly simplify your food drying:

Stainless steel knives

Glass, pottery, or stoneware bowls

Lightweight, nontoxic plastic wrap, or parchment paper (for drying liquids like soups, stews, leather, chili, or one-dish casseroles)

Bed sheets or cheesecloth (for making cottage cheese and cream cheese)

Scale for weighing up to 25 pounds (if you would like to know how much moisture your food lost during drying)

Meat Grinder

Blender

Food Slicer (not essential, but desirable)

Food or candy thermometer (for making yogurt)

Wooden cutting board

Slotted and wooden spoons

Kitchen shears (perfect for cutting dried foods)

Small end melon ball scoop

Shredder

Tomato Slicer

Cherry Pitter (for instructions on how to make your own, see page 68)

Apple parer and corer

Bean Stringer

OTHER METHODS

I was once a guest at a fair where large quantities of dried food were on display. Some people had sun-dried, some oven-dried, some obviously had used inferior commercial dehydrators or inferior homemade ones. All were displaying their wares with a great deal of pride and pleasure—until they had a chance to *see* the superior color and *taste* the fresh-like flavor of the fruits and vegetables I had dried.

I tell you all this because it clearly demonstrates what I have found to be true: the most superior way to dry is with a dependable pre-assembled home food dehydrator. It is the only kind I recommend to achieve the best results with the recipes in Chapters 9 and 10. I have already listed the desirable features to check. Besides buying one already preassembled, there are two other ways of acquiring a machine: through the purchase of a kit or building your own. Let me tell you what they both offer in the way of performance.

Kits

One of the reasons manufacturers prepare do-it-yourself kits is to satisfy those who long to have the satisfaction of putting a dehydrator together themselves, while at the same time protecting them from the struggles and disappointments of less desirable models. At least, they can begin with proper parts and proportions to complete a very professional model that dries food properly. Units will function completely satisfactorily if you follow directions carefully. Don't deviate. Otherwise, you are on your own. My favorite kit is a heavy wooden one (about 50 pounds), easy to assemble, with all the characteristics of a quality dehydrator.

Making Your Own

Not recommended. I am convinced that only a very small percentage of people can make a truly effective dehydrator (it's about equal to the same percentage of people who can put together a refrigerator that functions well). So much time is expended making, remaking, and perfecting it, they would have been wiser to have purchased a preassembled one right from the beginning. Finding usable parts and quality thermostats is a problem. Because of unreliable perform-ance, sometimes bags of food have been thrown away, making it economically unfeasible. There is considerable waste, and discontent-ment and discouragement about the whole food-drying process.

There is another dilemma—domestic tranquility. One woman who

attended one of my classes wanted to buy a dehydrator, but her husband had spent so many hours making one she said she was afraid
to hurt his feelings by complaining. His really did not work well at
all, and she was looking for some way of giving it away so she could
purchase a preassembled one. I couldn't blame her, for I have yet to
see a homemade dryer which turns out the flavor and color that a good
commercial one can. It certainly never will dry the great variety of
foods described in this book.

Now that I've said all that, if you still want to go ahead and make
your own, you are on your own. A good kit is a better way to go, and
if you follow the guidelines included earlier, you'll be assured of a
fine food-drying piece of equipment.

Sun-Drying

In the past (and even today) under relatively primitive conditions
people who sun-dried foods were fairly dependent on that particular
way of preserving. One must realize, however, that those people had
developed immunities over a period of time while eating that food,
thereby escaping the gastro-intestinal disturbances that may well lay
us low. Besides, their standards in terms of color, taste, nutrition,
and hygiene were far lower than ours.

Of course, the advantage to sun-drying is that it is cheap since the
sun's energy is there for anyone who cares to use it, but drying outdoors produces uncertain results and demands an enormous amount of
preprocessing that is not only time-consuming and laborious but

nutritionally substandard. If you use the recipes in this book (especially leathers, tomatoes, apricots) results cannot be guaranteed.

How to Sun-Dry. Not recommended, but if despite this good advice you want to go ahead and dry, you must be prepared to preblanch or steam food, put fruit into a saline or acid solution, and prepare an outside box or compartment to burn sulphur in the hope that the fumes (smoke) will prevent discoloration. All this before you even begin the job of actually drying. Needless to say, I must oversimplify because it is not in the scope of this book to give details on methods which do not produce the best results. However, let me give you the rest of the steps because there is more. You will need cloth-covered trays on which to place your preblanched, steamed, sulphured food. You can use either clean sheets, muslin, cheesecloth, or nylon netting. Trays and racks can be wooden or wire, or you may construct your own. Trays are then placed on tables, benches or some other support. A protecting cover, such as screen, nylon net, or cheesecloth is necessary to cover food to protect against insects, animals, or birds. Trays are placed in direct sun in an area free, hopefully, from dust and dirt. Food is turned once or twice a day in the hope that both sides will dry evenly. Trays are taken in at night to avoid evening dew, or covered and stacked in a sheltered area. Drying time varies according to weather conditions and size and thickness of food, and can take from six to sixteen days.

Pitfalls. Sun-drying has enough pitfalls to discourage its use. Perhaps the following reasons have led to its unpopularity in recent years.

1. The preprocessing that takes place: the chemical treatment with sulphur, and preblanching, lowers the nutritional values you are anxious to keep. The wide daily temperatures, from noontide heat to cold night air, cause fruit to discolor.

2. You must have ideal weather. Many days of sunny weather are required, about six to eight times longer than if a good commercial dryer is used (whose drying process doesn't depend on the weather). If you get just one foggy, cloudy, rainy day, you'll lose not only your whole crop but all your labor as well.

3. Many products take so long to dry that they virtually spoil before the drying process is completed. Thus, sun-drying of certain foods cannot even be attempted.

4. Food must be carried inside each night to protect it from the evening's dew and dampness.

5. Be prepared to battle birds, insects, flies, bees, and fruit flies who may eat or destroy your entire supply. (I remember that as a

youngster when we sun-dried, it was my job to sit by the drying apples and wave away the flies and birds. Tedious, tiresome, and not entirely successful.)

6. Since food must be left outdoors, it is exposed to smog, dust, soot, and a few other things you discover only with the passage of time. My students, for instance, have complained of little worms crawling out of dried food they dried in the sun and stored. Sun, combined with water, soil, and open air provide excellent breeding conditions for larvae that may already be in food, and inadequate and insufficient drying produces these unwelcome visitors.

Oven-Drying

Everyone owns an oven, so many people think they can overcome some of the disadvantages of sun-drying by using their ovens instead. It is another method that cannot do a proper job, but let's take a look at it anyway.

How to Oven-Dry. Not recommended. Preheat oven to very low temperature, 140 degrees or less. Check temperature at intervals to be sure it does not overheat. Prop doors open for entire drying time— anywhere from 1 to 8 inches (depending on whether you have a gas or electric oven). This allows moist air to escape. Trays must be about 1½ inches smaller than the inside of the oven. Allow at least 2 to 3 inches of space at top and bottom. Stretch cheesecloth over oven racks, pin, make as tight as possible, before placing food on trays so that both sides of food dry at same time. From time to time, food needs to be inspected and stirred so that food on edges is brought into the center of the tray. Examine for scorching toward end of drying time. Trays need to be rotated—from top to bottom, front to back. Drying time can take from 4 to 24 hours for vegetables, 10 to 48 hours for fruit, depending on juiciness, thickness, and temperature used.

Pitfalls. Here are five hazards of oven-drying:
1. An oven cannot maintain the proper low temperature needed—nor does it have a circulating system to adequately dry foods, so it cooks food instead of dehydrating it, drawing out the sugar content. This carmelization results in nutritional loss, darkens and discolors much of the food, and causes loss of fresh flavor.
2. There is no interior circulating system (all you can do is place a fan in front of the door) to move air over the food and out, taking the moist air with it.
3. The lack of air movement makes oven drying a very slow process, tying up your oven for hours, just to dry a few traysful of food. Not

only is this time-consuming and costly, but you can't use the oven for anything else.

4. Door must be left open a few inches. This is extremely expensive as energy escapes.

5. The long drying at this high temperature heats up your house.

WE'VE COME A LONG WAY

In days past, bread was toasted over an open flame and manual rotary eggbeaters were used to whip up cakes. Nobody dreams of doing that any more. Toasters do a much better job of toasting and electric mixers whip cake batter like grandma never dreamed possible. With the passage of time and the refinements of different appliances, newer and better pieces of equipment are being developed all the time to produce a more superior product. It is especially true in the field of food drying. The new age is dawning—the age of food drying, at home, in a dehydrator, the natural way. Enjoy it and live!

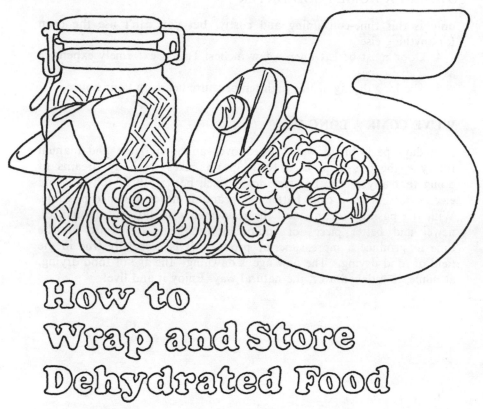

How to Wrap and Store Dehydrated Food

Now that you know how to achieve the proper degree of dryness and have prepared a quantity of dried food, it is essential that it be properly wrapped and stored to keep at maximum goodness for whatever length of time you choose. To help you understand the importance of this phase of the food-drying operation, let me tell you about one of my own experiences.

In my home at this moment, I have some apples which I dried sometime ago. They have been kept in the bottom cupboard of my kitchen, stored in a half-gallon, tightly-closed glass jar, in the recesses of a dark cloth bag. Ah, such care! But the reason is plain. The apples are a bit pinkish-beige in color, but the flavor is marvelous, and the apples are still nutritious.

Perhaps you see nothing exceptional in all this—but there is one remarkable fact: my dried apples are fifteen years old! If such careful storage is maintained, I can keep my apples another fifteen years. But longevity is really not the point I'm trying to make here. One season to the next is sufficient in which to keep dried food supplies, if you wish. My experiment simply demonstrates the importance of wrapping and storing dried food in the best possible way. That's what this chapter is all about.

NO DELAY

Once food is dry, there should be no delay in storing it, so even before beginning the task of washing and drying you should gather up the necessary containers. You must take foods off trays immediately. When the machine is turned off, dried food automatically begins to pick up moisture, gradually reconstituting itself to some degree, so your whole aim is directed toward keeping dried food dry. The extent to which this reconstitution takes place depends on the amount of moisture in the air. A high humidity climate, a home near the ocean or any body of water, or any place on a foggy or rainy day, will contribute to the reconstitution of food with great rapidity and might well cause mold later in storage if not redried. For this reason, it is wiser to dry indoors rather than outdoors in a garage or other outdoor area that tends toward dampness.

We all learn from experience. Before I put my dehydrator in the kitchen, I once dried cucumber slices in my garage. The slices were quite dry and crisp when I turned the dehydrator off just before leaving for the evening. When I returned, my once-crisp cucumber slices were moist and limp. At first, I couldn't understand how or why this happened. Then I realized one of those heavy Santa Monica fogs had crept in while I was away and reconstituted my slices. I saved them from molding by turning the dehydrator on once again, redrying and storing them before another fog could get at them.

But be assured that if your food is to be consumed within a short period of time, perhaps a few days, under normal circumstances there is no reason why it can't be left out. It may take you a while, as it did me, to adjust to seeing little bowls of tomato or banana slices "just sitting" around and not spoiling, but it is perfectly safe despite the fact that stowing them safely away in the refrigerator may seem safer. It is not. In fact, because of a refrigerator's high moisture content, it's entirely the worst thing to do.

PACKING

Airtight Packages. After testing to determine individual dryness (see Chapters 3, 8), place dehydrated slices and pieces into a glass jar, paper bag, plastic wrapper, or container. You want to achieve as airtight a state as possible. If using paper bag or plastic wrap, press out as much air as you can, and fold the edges over tightly before sealing. It's better to have food in your container rather than air, so fill it as full as possible without crushing your dried product.

One Item to a Container. If you are an individual or have a small family, you might have the sudden impulse to combine two food items (for example, dried apples and dried peaches) into one jar. Don't do it. Deny the impulse, for not only will flavor and odor pass from one fruit to another, but there are various degrees of dryness in fruits and vegetables (even though you have dried them as dry as possible) and the more moist one will pass its moisture content to the other.

Small Preferred. As to the matter of the container, consider using a variety of sizes no matter how small or large your family may be, because once a package is opened, it is best to eat the entire contents over a period of days rather than resealing and restoring.

I do recommend, however, preparing a large number of small, tempting packages (which you may then place into a larger outer bag or container). Then you can remove one small pack at a time, eating tasty morsels always at their best. There's another desirable feature to small packages. In the event a quantity spoils, no matter what the reason, you will have lost only one small package, rather than a larger amount. But by carefully reading and following the suggestions in this book, you should not have even this problem.

Naturally, larger containers may be used. It will depend entirely on the use you wish to make of the item itself. You may have a large family or want convenient, company-size packets. Just remember, there is the matter of contents reabsorbing moisture every time you open the lid to remove a portion of the food.

THE CONTAINER

I have prepared a list of suggested containers in the order of desirability. You will note many are already on your kitchen shelves. You can save them, or ask your friends to save theirs for your future use. The others are readily purchasable from local markets.

CONTAINERS IN ORDER OF DESIRABILITY

For Long-Term Storage—Two or Three Years or Longer

Glass Jars, Bottles. Canning jars, baby food, nut, pickle, honey, instant coffee, mayonnaise, and others of this order.

Brown Paper Bags. The kind groceries come in. All sizes. For long-term storage, place in tin or plastic-topped container, or cardboard carton.

Cloth Bags. Use old pillowcases, or make your own bags from closely woven material. For long-term storage, place in tin or plastic-topped container, or cardboard carton.

Cans. Coffee and shortening cans. Plastic-topped containers are not always airtight so pack food first in airtight bag.

Tins. Airtight cookie or cake tins.

For long-term shortage, I always recommend the Russian wooden egg procedure. As you open the large egg, you find another snugly sheltered within; pry that one apart, and you find another. This goes on and on until you find the tiniest and the last. I refer you back to the beginning of this chapter and the matter of my fifteen-year-old apples. If you tightly seal an item in a wrap and put that in a container within another container, your chances for maintaining peak quality for many years is practically assured. Unlike the Russian eggs, it's not a matter of surprise and discovery. It's just that the more airtight, dry, and light resistant you can keep the product, the better chance you'll have of choice, top-grade food. To repeat, for these lengthier periods, place paper-bagged items into a second paper or plastic bag, and then into a metal container, cardboard box, or carton. Such care is the best possible insurance against light, moisture, insects, or any other element that may cause a lesser product than what you so eagerly prepared and carefully packed.

For Short-Term Storage—A Few Weeks or a Few Months

Waterproof Nontoxic Plastic Bags. Heavy, durable bags. Plastic cooking pouches.

Plastic Containers. Good, food-grade, plastic refrigerator and freezer containers.

Plastic Wrap. Lightweight plastic wrap should be closed with rubber band or use package-wrap technique.

More on Containers

In case my list caused a brow to furrow, let me clarify a few things and offer a few cautions.

Glass Jars. Why are glass jars listed as most desirable? When tightly closed with their own lids, they are the best airtight containers. Glass jars can be washed and recycled, are practically bug-free, and contents are in plain view. Needless to say, be sure they are clean, and dry, dry, dry. However, unlike canning, one does not need to sterilize. A thorough washing in a dishwasher is adequate. One of my students was going to very carefully put all her filled glass jars through a steam bath to seal, as in canning. This would put steam into the dried food and hasten molding. Luckily, she told me first, and that particular problem was averted.

It is very important that the jar be thoroughly dry. Friends of mine who dehydrated large quantities of corn lost two containers out of the whole amount. The corn was from the same crop and dried the same length of time, so they were baffled until they remembered that the two jars in question were washed at the last minute and towel-dried. So when they immediately filled the jar with corn, evidently there was still just enough dampness left to cause the corn, stored over a long period of time, to mold.

Brown Bags. Are you surprised at their inclusion on the list? They do such a super job of absorbing moisture and keeping out light. They take up less space than bottles, are free from chemical-inducing diseases now associated with certain types of plastic, are easily obtainable and—a small but welcome benefit— you can mark contents right on the wrapper.

Cloth Bags. It is interesting to note that early pioneers used to store their dried food in old pillowcases. If you're reluctant to tackle yardage shops and sewing machines to stitch up a supply, just use worn pillowcases instead. They make excellent wrappers because moisture and light do not easily penetrate the interior.

Plastic. Read the label. Purchase plastic that does not list polyvinyl chloride in the manufacturing process. This is the chemical currently being identified as a possible cause of birth defects, cancer, and other diseases. For short-term storage or for taking dried foods along for travel or backpacking, plastic is fine. But since we don't know what the end result of the testing may be, it would be wise if you are planning to store food for long periods to use some other container or wrap instead, and not place dried food right next to plastic itself.

Another characteristic of plastic you should be aware of is that some types are porous. Moisture can enter, causing first some discoloration of dried food, and then mold. The heavier, more durable, waterproof quality is the type you should buy.

Now that you know all this, I'd like to balance the argument by telling you the plus factors of plastic. Unlike glass, it does not break, it is lightweight (important to consider in traveling or backpacking), takes up less space, and creates airtight, compact, see-through packages.

How to Close

Jars. Jars come conveniently with their own tight-fitting lids. Many have an excellent innerseal, such as airsealed nut jars. If your lids are of poor quality, local supermarkets carry replacements in several sizes.

Paper or Cloth Bags. Wrap and fold tightly over food to eliminate as much air as you can. Tape with masking tape or use string or rubber band. For long-term storage, you should put the packs into another container, such as a glass jar, metal tin, or cardboard carton.

Plastic Wrap. Wrap and fold tightly to eliminate air. Close either with masking tape, twister seal, string, or rubber band.

Plastic Container. Look for those that are airtight with airtight covers.

THE LABEL

What's in a name? Plenty. Spare yourself any unexpected surprises. Your water might boil away as you hunted through oregano, comfrey, and chive bags before you found the one with the mint tea, so carefully identify each package. If packed in a paper bag, write directly on it with a felt pen. If in a bottle, metal container, or plastic container, stationers and dime stores carry assortments of gummed and pressure-sensitive labels.

To the usual facts (date and name of item), you might wish to prepare a little history in order to refine your drying process. Re-create the moment of preparation and put down whose orchard the fruit came from, or from which store you purchased it, or which seeds you used in growing it in your garden. You might include variations in the process: length of drying time, thickness of cut. Your little record, therefore, might read something like this: "Peaches from Aunt Bee's orchard. 2 pounds fresh. Sliced with peel ¼ inch thick. Dried August, 1976 for 8½ hours."

It might be prudent to prepare labels ahead of time if you're using brown paper bags since one bag looks just like another, and in minutes you can forget whether you packed strips of jerky or zucchini.

DIFFERENCES IN STORAGE

Does the way you pack really make any difference in the end? Yes, it does, as you will see from this story of a supply of pears I once dried. The pears, which had come from the same tree, had grown big, golden, and juicy in a sunny fruit orchard. I divided my dried slices into two, packed half in a plastic bag, the other half in glass jars, and stored them in my garage.

Some time later when I took samples from both containers, this was the result: The plastic-bagged pears had turned a beige-brown color. Texture and flavor had diminished because moisture had seeped into the plastic (both because plastic is porous and garages are damp). The ones in the glass jars, however, had retained their beautiful, golden color with texture and flavor intact.

Today, I have a wide variety of fruits and vegetables stored in my kitchen (not the garage), packed airtight in glass jars or in brown paper bags, and enclosed in tins or cartons. Although it's well over a year when I last checked, they were still bright in color, retaining the concentrated flavor and lovely texture that's so desirable.

It's a recurring question, this matter of how long dehydrated food should be kept. My fifteen-year-old dry apples are only modest examples. Suffice it to say that dried food, if kept in an airtight container in a cool, dry, dark spot, will keep indefinitely— though I doubt that flavor and nutrition improve with age. And after all, why should you plan such lengthy storage since you will undoubtedly wish to add to your dried food supply each season from the assortment of fresh fruits and vegetables available.

How to Store

If you are planning to eat a dried product within a few weeks to two or three months, you'll want to pack it a bit differently than if you are storing it for two or three years, or longer. To give you an idea of the range of possibilities, let us take one product, say, fruit leather, as an example:

To Store for One Month or Longer. Roll up each roll on wrap. Close and twist ends.

To Store for One to Two Years. Remove leathers from wrap and store flat with sheets of brown paper between each layer. Place in a rectangular, airtight cardboard box or tin, and cover. Seal with tape.

To Store Over Two Years. Remove leathers from plastic wrap or parchment. Roll into rolls, place lengthwise (you may wish to cut into one- or two-inch pieces) into tall glass jars. Close with tight lid or cork and store in a cool, dry, dark place.

Three Criteria of Storage

There are three simple words to remember when storing dehydrated foods. Dry, cool, and dark. The insistence on dry, cool, dark places for storage cannot be stressed enough.

Dry. I once had a student call who wanted to share with me her initial food-drying experiences. In the happy belief that she was following the storage instructions, she had carefully wrapped and stored her precious supply of dehydrated food in the refrigerator. Her obvious delight filled me with dismay, and I wasted no time in telling her that her great care was placed in the wrong institution. She failed to realize that her dried foods would soon pick up all that moist refrigerator air—terrific for fresh foods, disaster for dried. So please, like Chiquita banana says, no long-term storage in the refrigerator.

Although a refrigerator is a poor choice, a freezer is a good (but not necessary) choice. Now why should this be so? Because dried food is practically free of water, and in an airtight container food can be frozen satisfactorily. This is especially true if you underdry and want to have soft, chewy fruits or vegetables.

Cool. Well, now, just how cool is cool? The ideal is about 50 to 80 degrees, or about room temperature. But since food was dried at 118 degrees, chances are it would not spoil if on rare occasions storage area temperature went to 118 degrees.

Dark. In addition to coolness and dryness, a dark area is desirable. Deterioration, fading, and browning result when dried food is left in bright sun or any lighted area. I found this out the hard way. I had a jarful of dried cabbage that was three years old, beautifully green, with a fragrant aroma. It tasted great. I was so proud of it that I began carrying it around with me in my car to use at my lectures as a marvelous demonstration of its aesthetic and wholesome durability. Of course, in the car it was exposed to sun. After a few days, the wonderful fragrance disappeared, the green faded to beige and, to my consternation, I was left with a jarful of unappetizing stuff. It was not spoiled; it had just deteriorated into a colorless, odorless, nutritionless, unappealing mass, certainly nothing which I could any longer show off with pride to my students. So, the moral of the story is that although sunflowers, trees, and daisies thrive in the sun and although it provides humans with a measure of vitamin D, sun does not have a salutary effect on dried foods.

Some good storage areas, in order of preference, are: low shelves in closets, cupboards, or pantries; under beds (a perfect spot); dry cellars (on the West Coast or in desert areas), but off cement floors since cement holds moisture. Just put down a simple riser—boards or plywood ought to do—and put your packages on top of that; an attic (but only if it is dry and cool). Just remember, for long storage, it should not get above room temperature. If the room available is in a sunlit area, simply darken not your brow but your jars. You can cover them with foil, dark plastic, or yardage, or you can put them into paper bags.

Inspect and Rotate

Once food is stored, check it every few days in the beginning, then every week until two months have passed, then once a month. Here is what you look for:

Moisture. Shake the container. If food sticks together instead of separating easily, it is just not dry enough. Test also the bag or plastic-wrapped packages. Open. If stuck together or if pieces stick together when pressed, spread once more on trays and dry again.

Insects. In all my years of drying, I have never had a single incident of small insects, ants, or any other living creature (outside of the appropriate two-legged humans) getting at my supplies. I believe this is due to correct drying and storing.

This is another reason I do not believe that the garage is the best place in which to store dehydrated food. Cars, yes. Food, no.

Rotation. Work out a plan for your supplies. If tomatoes are in short supply one season, you might wish to keep some over for the next. But always use the first supply dried before beginning on the second.

THE LAST WORD

To underscore for the last time the need for dry, airtight containers stored in cool, dark, dry storage areas, let me conclude with this incident. We must go back in time to the olden days when Egyptians buried their dead in the Pyramids. Upon opening one such tomb, along with the pottery, jewelry, and body of an ancient ruler, archeologists came upon some intact kernels of wheat. In the interest of science, the men decided to plant the wheat. Within a matter of weeks, the tiny grains of wheat placed in that tomb thousands of years ago, and now planted in the rich, moist Egyptian soil, germinated, took root, and grew!

Need anything more be said about the life force that can be kept dormant in matter if it is properly stored in a cool, dark, dry place?

Using Your Dehydrator All Year Long

There's nothing more wonderful than having an appliance do its work well and then find out it has the happy capacity to carry out a dozen other functions. This is true of your home food dehydrator. It won't vacuum your rugs or wash your dishes, but it will perform a number of food services quietly, efficiently, healthfully, economically, deliciously all year long.

How?

Let me count the ways so you'll be sure to take advantage of them all. The majority fall mostly into four categories: Chapters 7, 8, 9, 10. There are other uses I would like to tell you about, but let us begin first with the chapters.

Chapter 7—For Brown Baggers, Purse Packers, and Backpackers. Dried foods and recipes are categorized for ease in taking meals and snacks along with you.

Chapter 8—How to Dry Fruits and Vegetables. Gives you tips on drying and buying. Ways of cutting. Instructions on reconstituting.

Chapter 9—Tempting Concoctions to Make in Your Dryer. You'll marvel at how wholesomely delicious they all are; crisp chips for snacks or dips; crunchy, whole-grain crackers; nibbles and nuts; turkey, beef, and fish jerky; the best pasta outside of Italy (using freshly ground grains and dried, powdered vegetables); multiple fruits and vegetable leathers (that wonderful misnamed delicacy made from pureed fruits or vegetables).

This chapter may hold a few other surprises for you. For instance:
Did you know that your dehydrator is the perfect place to let yeast dough rise for breads, rolls, and coffee cakes if you remove the bottom four trays and place dough on bottom of dehydrator?
Did you know that it is possible to prepare fresh-tasting, homemade jam without using a trace of sugar?
Did you know that if a commercially prepared cereal has become stale and soft, you give it the lift it needs with a few hours or overnight in the dehydrator? Or better yet, you can put together your own delicious mixture using grains of your own choice.
Did you know that yogurt, cream cheese, and cottage cheese can be made overnight with just a few ingredients?
Most remarkable of all, did you know that your dehydrator can help your pet eat better too!

Chapter 10—Recipes Using Home-Dried Foods. There are many to choose from, including Orange Glazed Pork Chops, Devilishly Good Pizza, Colorful Zucchini, Cream of Mushroom Soup, Pineapple Cabbage Slaw, Bourbon Pecan Cake, and Cherry Ice Cream.
All of the above items can be found in the Index.

And . . . other adventures await you, too. You may need an ocean or garden, or simply nothing more than an extra dozen eggs or leftover chili. I list them below alphabetically rather than include them in the chapters that follow since they seem to defy any other arrangement. (Remember to use the recommended low temperature of 110 degrees to 118 degrees.)
Now with all this before you, it is my hope that you will find pleasure upon pleasure in this marvelous world of food drying.

Buds, Blossoms, and Flowers

Edible blossoms, flowers, and buds may all be dried. Place clean, dry blossoms (orange, apple, strawberry, pear, honeysuckle, or peach) on dehydrator trays one layer thick. Dry until brittle, from 2 to 7 hours. Store blossoms whole; crush before using for tea or for salad. Rose hips may be dried for their vitamin content. Dried flowers and buds (geranium, nasturtium, violet, rose petals) may be crushed for use in salad or are delightful dried for their beauty alone. Surprisingly, they not only retain beautiful colors but also aroma and make wonderfully fragrant sachets.

Croutons

Cut bread into ½-inch cubes. Place on dehydrator trays. Dry until desired crispness, 3 to 8 hours.

Eggs

Eggs may be dried (cooked or raw). Line trays with plastic wrap or parchment paper, taping each corner to tray with transparent or masking tape to prevent lining from blowing over eggs.

If Cooked. Hardcook eggs in shell. Cool in cold water. Remove shell. *Whites*—Chop and place on lined tray. Dry about 8 to 10 hours until very hard and translucent in appearance. To reconstitute, cover with water, soak overnight (refrigerated). Drain. Use in making tuna, chicken, meat salad, or creamed eggs. *Yolks*—Chop and place on lined tray. Dry about 8 to 10 hours until crumbly and easily broken apart with hands. If desired, powder in blender. To store: egg yolks contain some fat and will store only about 3 or 4 weeks before they begin to turn a little rancid. To keep longer, freeze. Dried cooked egg yolks that have been powdered in blender can be used in baking cakes and cookies, or mixed in or sprinkled over the top of potato or meat salad, creamed eggs.

If Raw. Blend 4 eggs in blender or beat by hand. Pour or spread on a lined tray in a rectangular shape about ¼-inch thick as for making a leather. Dry about 24 hours or until eggs pull away from liner easily and break into pieces. Yield: 1 cup pieces which, when powdered in blender, become ½ cup powdered egg. (To store, see above.)

Herbs

Herbs are easy to grow in gardens or in pots on windowsills and even easier to dry. Pick and wash in cool water. Shake off moisture. Blot dry. Place on trays 2½ to 10 hours or until dry enough so that leaves crush easily. They retain better flavor if kept whole, uncrushed, until ready to use. A few of the many that can be dried for seasoning and flavoring are bay leaf, celery tops, chives (chopped or snipped), dill, green onion tops (chopped or snipped), mint, oregano, parsley, sage.

Leftovers (Chilis, Stews, One-Dish Meals, Soups)

No need to waste a single morsel. Line tray with plastic wrap or parchment paper; tape each corner to tray with transparent tape. Remove fat from meat dishes. Spread food ¼- to ⅜-inch thick on lined tray, cutting any chunks or large pieces into ¼-inch thick slices. Dry until almost dry. Peel away from wrap. Discard wrap. Place food back on tray and continue drying. When dry, break apart and store. Most foods just need the addition of water before heating to reconstitute. For others, pour 1 cup warm or hot water over 1 cup food in a narrow, high-walled container so that water covers food. Let soak 30 minutes to 2 hours, or overnight. Heat and eat.

Meats

Raw Meat. It would be worth owning a good home dehydrator just to make jerky. Drying methods given are for making various kinds, such as beef, turkey, and fish. (See Index.) Other raw meat does not reconstitute well, and raw pork should never be dried.

Cooked Meat. Beef, veal, pork, lamb, chicken, turkey, fish, shrimp, clams, seafood are all easy to dry. Slice ⅛- to ¼-inch thick across grain. Butterfly shrimp. Place on trays and dry 5 to 7 hours or until hard and brittle. To reconstitute, pour 1 cup hot water over 1 cup sliced, dried meat. Let soak 1 or 2 hours or overnight or until soft. Cook by usual method, adding bouillon to increase flavor, if desired. Heat if making a hot sandwich or use cold in a meat salad.

Seaweed

Those who live in coastal regions can lie in the sun, swim in the surf, and then come home bringing back a tidy bit of seaweed to dry. Stems and bulbs are excellent for making Salt Substitute, (see Index.) Wash off algae. Cut in 12- to 18-inch pieces, and place on trays for 5 to 7 hours or until leaves are crisp, stems and bulbs dry. Powder in blender for kelp.

Seeds .

The seeds of most fruits and vegetables (apricots, pumpkin, watermelon, sunflower) dry extremely well. What you don't care to eat, you can store and use for your next year's garden. Wash seeds. Place on trays one layer thick. Dry 5 to 8 hours or overnight or until quite brittle.

Teas

Leaves of your favorite edible plant or tree (strawberry, lemon, orange, apple, cherry, alfalfa, clover, mint, comfrey) can be dried to make a fine, hot brew. Wash leaves. Let them dry well. Place on trays and dry until brittle, 2 to 7 hours. Store leaves whole to retain more flavor. Crush just before using or blend together to make your own combination of herb tea. Use 1¼ teaspoons crushed leaves in one cup of very hot water. Cover. Steep for 3 minutes. Strain and serve with cream or lemon and honey.

TO THE INQUIRING READER

Much testing and experimentation have gone into this book which covers an entirely new method of drying food the natural way. It will be updated and revised as new information becomes available. If you would care to share your ideas and recipe suggestions, please write to me at 1154 Roberto Lane, Los Angeles, California 90024. In addition, I would be happy to supply information on where and how to purchase food dehydrators; food grinders or mills; grains, raw nuts, seeds; slicers and cutting equipment. Send a stamped, self-addressed envelope with your request. *—Bee Beyer*

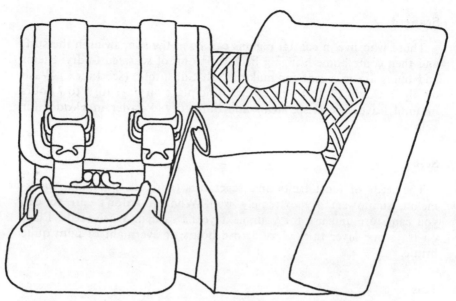

For Brown Baggers, Purse Packers, and Backpackers

You will love the benefits of dried foods if you are a backpacker, brown bagger, vacationer or traveler, or just off for the day to some remote beach. The only packing materials needed are lightweight plastic wrap and/or paper bags to pack individual or group portions. If you are a fisherman or spend much time around water, you might want waterproof material in which to pack your foods depending on your length of stay.

As you can see, most of this is hand-to-mouth food, eaten as it is, straight from the bag. Some need the barest of extras, such as water and a paper cup. They are all easy, good-traveling, take-along foods. Page numbers of individual recipes are listed in the Index.

EATEN OUT OF HAND WITH NO ADDITION OF WATER

Complete Meals. Healthy Meal in a Snack.

Meats. Beef (Beef Jerky, Beef Jerky Sticks, Beef Jerky with Chili, Favorite Beef Jerky, Tacos, Tasty Beef Sticks). Fish (Dried Butterfish or Catfish, Dried Fish, Dried Turbot, Tuna Chip Snacks). Poultry (Chicken Snacks, Jerky made from Turkey, Turkey Snacks).

Cereals. Granola, Health Cereal.

Crackers. Honey Graham Crackers, Sesame Wheat Crackers.

Snacks. Corn Tomato Chips, Fresh Corn Chips, Homemade Raisins, Nuts, Raisin Peanut Snack.

Dried Vegetables. Beets, cabbage, carrots (grated), cauliflower, cucumber chips, green peppers, sprouts, tomato chips, zucchini chips.

Dried Fruits. Apples, apricots, avocados, bananas, dark sweet cherries, dates, grapefruits, raisins (grapes), lemons, limes, melons, oranges, papayas, peaches and nectarines, pears, persimmons, pineapples, prunes (plums), strawberries.

Leathers. All varieties, fruit or vegetable.

Cookies and Bars. Apple Cookies, Coconut Granola Bars, Coconut Pineapple Almond Diamonds, Heavenly-Fruit Bars, Persimmon Cookies, Persimmon Oatmeal Drop Cookies, Pumpkin Date Bars, Special Oatmeal Cookies, Three-Layer Fruit Bars.

IF YOU HAVE WATER, A STIRRER, AND PAPER CUP

Juices. Orange juice, Tomato juice.

IF YOU HAVE HEAT, SPOON FOR STIRRING, POT OR FRY PAN, OIL, A DISH, EATING SPOON, NONFAT DRY MILK, AND A CONTAINER.

Complete Meals. Chicken or Turkey Noodle Dinner, Corned Beef and Rice, Yum Yum Spaghetti.

Fruits. Reconstituted Fruit for Breakfast, Dessert, Salad, or Side Dish.

Cereals. Grind and measure cereals ahead (Four-Grain Cereal, Seven-Grain Cereal, Wheat Raisin Cereal).

Eggs. Plain Omelet, Cheese-Tomato Omelet, Scrambled Eggs.

Soups. Easy Beef Vegetable Soup, A Cup of Soup, Cream of Spinach Soup and all the variations (if you want to omit the butter, substitute 2/3 cup nonfat dry milk powder and 1¾ cups water for raw milk and half and half). Easy Tomato Soup, Tomato Beef Soup, Tomato Rice Soup.

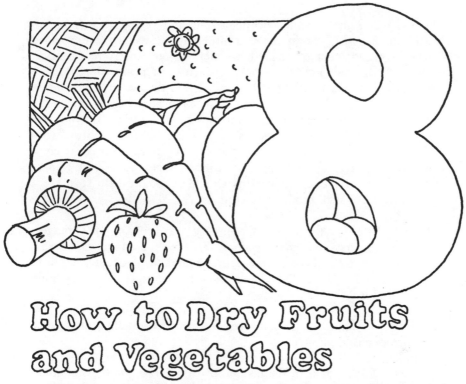

How to Dry Fruits and Vegetables

(If you began reading this book from the first page, this paragraph will sound repetitious since the material was covered earlier. I summarize it here for the benefit of those who are reading this section first because they want to get right down to drying that bagful of cherries or box of mushrooms in their kitchen.)

Fruits and vegetables should be dehydrated when they are at peak of ripeness or perfection. If they taste best in the fresh state, they will taste best in their dried state. Do not dry green or underripe foods and expect them to taste any way but green or underripe. By the same token, overripe and bruised fruit will come out of the dehydrator overripe and bruised. That which goes into the dehydrator tough or stringy will come out the same way. Fruits will taste sweeter due to the concentration of the natural fruit sweetness although no sugar has been added. Dried vegetables may taste as if they have been salted, although no salt has been added because the natural salt is now concentrated. Pick quality foods for eating as well as for drying. Price has nothing to do with quality; these factors do:

1. **Depth of color.** The deeper the natural color, the better the flavor and nutrition. Cabbage or lettuce which is green is better than that

which is very light or almost white. Fruits and vegetables allowed to "ripen on the vine," or in their natural habitat will have developed more flavor and nutrition than those picked prematurely to transport to market. Did you ever buy apples, peaches, or pears which looked very appetizing only to get them home and find they were brown inside or around the core? These fruits have been picked before they were ripe, stored at a low temperature, and passed on to you. Not only are they tasteless, pithy, and brown inside, but they do not improve with drying. The best way to eliminate the practice is to return this cold-storage fruit to the produce buyer or store manager, cut the fruit open, and ask for your money back. This should gradually help to prevent the passing on of such products to consumers.

2. **Feel.** Often you can feel the greasy wax coating on oranges, apples, cucumbers, and green pepper. This wax contains chemicals. Water sprayed over them in the store will cling together in little droplets, and if you run hot water over the product, you'll be able to detect and feel the wax.

3. **Smell.** Chemicals can often be detected by smelling the calyx or surface opposite the stem.

4. **Taste.** The proof is in the taste and eating. The goodness of some foods, such as melons, can only be proven by tasting. Tasteless food has little nutrition or appeal.

5. **Choose foods in season.** Foods in season are cheaper. This is the time to dry them for later use. "Ripened-on-the-vine" foods develop more flavor and nutrition, so dry at peak of ripeness and flavor and not when green or overripe.

APPLES

A great variety of apples are grown in various parts of the country and at different seasons of the year making some available almost year round. Contrary to popular belief, Golden Delicious, not Red Delicious, is the favorite. (Rodger P. Hall, an elementary teacher in Columbus, Missouri, discovered this after testing 7000 fifth-and sixth-grade students over the past twelve years: 50 percent preferred the Golden Delicious apple, 40 percent the Jonathan, only 10 percent the Red Delicious.) Golden Delicious dry beautifully and do not dis-

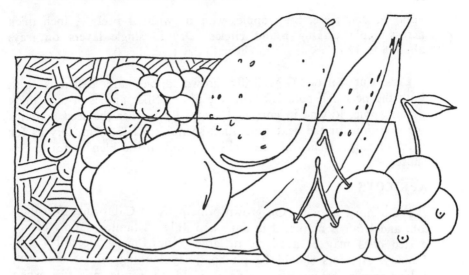

color if dried properly. Begin with tree-ripened, firm, crisp, well-colored apples. Cold storage apples will probably turn brown when dried. Unfortunately, commercial apples are often waxed to enhance beauty and increase sales. There is no way this wax usually loaded with preservatives can be washed off. If this is the case, peel. Did you ever bite or cut into an apple and eat only part leaving the rest at room temperature or refrigerated only to find that days later it had not even discolored? That apple was injected with many chemicals so if you purchase organically grown ones you can enjoy added nutrition of peel (which is good for you) as well as the seeds.

Slices. Slice apples, with or without peel, into ¼-inch-thick slices. Arrange in a single layer on trays. Dry 8 to 12 hours or overnight, until beyond the bendable and leathery stage. Completely dried apples will snap or break when bent. The sweeter the apple, the longer the drying time required. Dried apples make good snacks or may be added without being reconstituted to cereals, pancakes, waffles, breads, cookies, cakes, stuffing.

To Reconstitute. Place ½ cup apples in narrow high-walled container so that 1/3 cup warm water will almost cover them; soak in refrigerator or at room temperature 30 minutes to 2 hours, or refrigerate overnight until soft. Yield: ½ cup plus 1½ tablespoons. To make applesauce, puree ½ cup apples in blender with ½ cup water. Yield: ½ cup sauce for use in recipes or to eat as applesauce.

Rings. Use an apple or pear corer to remove center core, leaving apple in one piece. Slice apple, with or without peel, ¼ inch thick across apple making round circles. Dry in single layers on trays about 8 to 12 hours or overnight until dry (see Slices).

Cross-Cut Slices. Organically grown apples are delicious with both the peel and core left with the apple. Slice apples ¼-inch thick across apple, leaving in core and seeds. Remember the seed contains the nutrition for the next generation so don't waste them. Dry as for slices or rings. Delicious as snacks or puree in the blender for applesauce.

APRICOTS

The bumper apricot crop grown principally in California, Washington, and Utah is marketed in June and July. A limited supply of imported ones may be available in larger cities during December and January. Apricots should be plump, juicy looking, and a uniform, golden-orange color. Ripe apricots yield to gentle pressure when pressed. Avoid overly mature, dull-looking, soft, or mushy fruit, as well as immature, very firm, pale yellow, or greenish-yellow fruit. Select firm, ripe fruit, no need to peel.

Drying apricots in the sun takes days with much chasing of flies, fruit flies, and dirt, not to mention birds and rain which usually cause loss of the whole crop. Sun-dried apricots eventually turn black and are the kind found in health food stores at a premium price. I perfer these black sun-dried apricots to the commercial ones which are usually preblanched and sulphured with chemicals. With a really quality home dehydrator, you'll have beautiful results without preservatives.

Slices. Cut into ¼-inch-thick slices; arrange in single layer on trays. Dry 7 to 10 hours or until fairly hard but chewable. These thin slices, when properly stored, will retain a beautiful color from one season to the next or even longer. They're wonderful as snacks, or may be added, without being reconstituted, to cereals, pancakes, waffles, breads, and cookies.

To Reconstitute. Place ½ cup apricots in narrow high-walled container so that ½ cup warm water will almost cover them. Soak in refrigerator or at room temperature 1 or 2 hours, or refrigerate overnight, until soft. Eat as fresh. Yield: ½ cup plus 1½ tablespoons of apricots.

To make an apricot sauce, puree ½ cup apricots and ½ cup water in blender. Yield: ½ cup sauce for making puddings, pies, breads, apricot butter.

Squishing. After preparing 160 pounds of apricots, my children named this process from the squishing sound the apricots made when pressed to ¼ inch thickness. Place apricot halves on a board or hard surface, skin side up. Gently press with palm of the hand, rolling pin, or pancake turner to ¼ inch thickness. Slide turner under apricot halves and turn over on dehydrator trays (skin side down). Dry about 12 to 14 hours until hard but chewable.

To Reconstitute. Use same procedure as for slices.

Halves. Place halves skin side down on dehydrator trays. Dry approximately 16 to 18 hours or until hard but chewable.

Glazed Halves. Dip halves in a mixture of approximately ½ cup honey and ½ cup water. Since the thickness of honey varies, it is difficult to give exact amounts, but mixture should be about the consistency of syrup. Drain halves in colander to remove excess syrup. Arrange on trays and dry about 48 hours (2 days) or until dry but still chewable. Halves will have a beautiful, shiny, lasting color, whereas unglazed halves or squished halves may darken very slightly after 9 to 12 months.

AVOCADOS

Avocados from California or Florida are available year round. Since they have a high fat content, dried avocados become rancid quickly and should be stored only for short periods (about one month). Freezing carefully packaged dried avocados enables them to be kept longer by greatly slowing down the development of rancidity.

Slices. Remove seed and peel and cut avocado in ¼-inch-thick slices. Arrange on trays. Dry 18 to 24 hours or until hard. Avocados will break when bent.

To Reconstitute. Avocado slices will discolor slightly, but when placed in a blender to make a guacamole dip or salad dressing, the inside green color returns. Puree ½ cup broken pieces of dried avocado with ½ cup hot water and ½ cup yogurt or sour cream. Add about 1 tablespoon lemon juice. Additional seasoning, such as powdered onion or garlic, will enhance the flavor.

BANANAS

Bananas, unlike most other fruit, develop their best eating quality after they are harvested. This allows them to be shipped great distances. Available year round, bananas are supplied almost entirely from Central and South America. They should not be refrigerated as they are sensitive to, and injured at, cool temperatures below 55 degrees. The ideal temperature to ripen them is 60 to 70 degrees; higher temperatures cause them to ripen too rapidly. The best flavor and eating quality of bananas has been reached when the solid yellow color is specked with brown. The flesh is mellow and the flavor is fully developed. At this stage, the banana needs to be eaten or used immediately; it is now perfect for drying. Occasionally, the skin may be entirely brown; but the flesh will be in prime condition.

When I dry bananas, I place two trays side by side. One is for drying the banana slices of the completely light part of the banana; the second is lined with plastic wrap or parchment paper for fruit leather. The part of the banana which is a little dark or bruised but definitely not spoiled goes into fruit leathers. Bananas combine beautifully with most other fruit for fruit roll or leathers.

Slices. Cut into ¼-inch-thick slices; arrange in single layers on dehydrator trays. Place each tray in dehydrator as it is filled or banana slices will begin to darken before reaching dehydrator. Dry 12 to 16 hours or until dry but chewable. Excellent as a snack instead of candy, or they may be added, without being reconstituted, to cereal (they'll become soft but chewy in the milk), cake, pie, cookies, pancakes, waffles, breads, fruit compote, and gelatine. Many people purchase a quality dehydrator just to make banana slices or chips, which are much better tasting and nutritious than commercially prepared ones that have generally been dipped in a sugar and/or honey mixture and heated to a high temperature.

Dipping. ¼-inch-thick slices may be dipped in naturally sweet pineapple juice for variety. Dry in single layers 24 to 30 hours or until dry but chewable.

To Reconstitute. Place ½ cup banana slices in narrow, high-walled container so that ½ cup water will almost cover them. Soak in refrigerator or at room temperature 1 or 2 hours, or refrigerate overnight, until soft. Bananas will taste fresh but will not be very attractive. For this reason, it is best to reconstitute them with other fruit or puree them in the blender to make a sauce for use in breads, cake, pie, cookies, puddings, and ice cream. Yield: ½ cup plus 1½ tablespoons banana puree for use in recipes calling for mashed banana or banana puree. Dried bananas may be pureed in blender with water without reconstituting first.

Chips. Slice banana ⅛ inch thick or as thin as possible, perhaps using an electric slicer. Dry in single layers until very crisp—about 8 to 12 hours. Serve as a snack.

Cut Lengthwise in Half. Arrange cut side up on trays and dry approximately 2 days (48 hours) until dry but chewy. These bananas will not keep as long as slices or chips (which I prefer) but are tasty as quick snacks.

BERRIES

Blueberries are on the market from May through September. A dark-blue color with a silvery bloom is the best indication of quality.

Cranberries are available in large quantity from September through January. Berries should be plump with a lustrous color.

Strawberries are in greatest supply in May and June. Berries should have a full red color and a bright luster, firm flesh, and the cap stem still attached. Medium to small strawberries generally have better eating quality than large ones. Raspberries, boysenberries, blackberries, dewberries, loganberries and youngberries are similar in general structure. They should have a clean bright appearance and uniform good color. Individual cells which make up the berry should be plump and tender, but not mushy. Avoid leaky or moldy berries.

Slices, Halves, Whole Berries. Cut blueberries and cranberries in half to dry. Strawberries may be cut in half, but they dry best when cut in ¼-inch thick pieces. Many berries can be dried whole. Blueberries and cranberries require about 8 to 12 hours drying. Strawberry halves may take about 20 hours to dry, and ¼-inch slices dry in approximately 16 hours. Whole raspberries, boysenberries, blackberries, dewberries, loganberries, and youngberries take from 20 to 36 hours to dry.

To Reconstitute. Soak ½ cup berries in ½ cup warm water 1 or 2 hours or overnight. Use as fresh or puree for sauce. Equal amounts of dried berries and water may be pureed in the blender without soaking to make a sauce that can be used for shakes, in yogurt, over pudding or ice cream, and for other cooking purposes.

CHERRIES

Naturally sweet cherries are produced in our western states from May through August. Sour red, tart cherries used mainly in pie or cooked desserts have softer flesh, lighter red color, and tart flavor. A very dark color is a sign of good flavor and nutrition in sweet cherries such as Bing, Black Tartarian, Schmidt, Chapman, and Republican varieties which range from deep maroon or mahogany red to black when richest in flavor. Overmature cherries which are shriveled with dried stems and a dull appearance generally lack flavor.

Purchasing a cherry pitter is quite an asset. You can also make your own. Purchase a small stainless steel broiler pan with rounded holes slightly larger than cherry stones. If holes are too small, they may be drilled larger. Hunt for a 5- to 6-inch long, round ⅜-inch thick plastic cylinder or cocktail stirrer. (We located one at a plastic-producing plant among the scraps.) Heat the end of the plastic cylinder and press against a flat surface to make a blunt end. Place washed, stemmed cherries centered above each hole on tray of broiler pan with stem side up. Place blunt end of plastic stick on cherry; press down so that pit goes through and below top tray of broiler pan. Seeds collect below, pitted cherries stay on top of tray.

Halves. Cherries, especially sweet ones, dry best when pitted and cut in half. Place in single layers on dehydrator trays. Dry approximately 24 to 30 hours, depending on sweetness and size of cherries. Sweeter cherries, as true of other fruits, require a longer drying period than tart ones. Bing and other sweet cherries are so delicious eaten as snacks that it almost seems a misuse to put them to any other purpose. They can be added, without being reconstituted, to ice cream, cake, and breads, or may be reconstituted and eaten for breakfast or dessert.

To Reconstitute. Place ½ cup cherries in narrow high-walled container so that ½ cup warm or hot water will almost cover them. Soak in refrigerator or at room temperature 1 or 2 hours, or refrigerate overnight, until soft. Eat as a breakfast fruit or dessert or puree in blender for sauce over ice cream. Yield: ½ cup plus 1½ tablespoon sauce; ½ cup dried cherries and ½ cup water may also be pureed in blender without soaking for a sauce.

DATES

Fresh dates, which are naturally sweet, combine well with other fruits and can replace the need for sugar.

Halves. Cut in half, remove seeds, arrange on trays. Dry 24 to 36 hours or until dates do not stick together when stored. They will always be slightly sticky. Use as a snack, in cereal, in baking, and combined with other fruits.

FIGS

Of the many varieties of light and dark figs, the light ones seem to dry best.

Quarter Slices. Peel figs and cut in quarters. Dry on trays 10 to 12 hours or until fairly hard but chewable.

To Reconstitute. Place ½ cup figs in narrow high-walled container so that ½ cup warm water will cover them. Let soak 1 or 2 hours at room temperature, or refrigerate overnight, until soft. Use in making cookies, pie, or cake. Figs and water may be pureed in blender without soaking.

GRAPEFRUIT

Although available year round, abundant supplies are from January through May. Most grapefruit is from Florida, others are from Texas, California, and Arizona. Grapefruit may be "seedless" (having no or few seeds) or seeded with white, pink, or red flesh. Fruit should be firm, heavy for its size. Thin-skinned grapefruit are juicier than coarse-skinned fruit. If pointed at the stem end, it is likely to be thick-skinned.
To dry, see "Oranges."

GRAPES

Most common grapes are of the European type, grown mostly in California. These firm-fleshed, generally high sugar content, are Thompson seedless (an early green grape), Tokay and Cardinal (early bright red grapes), and Emperor (late, deep red grape). When mature, all have an excellent flavor. Softer flesh American-type grapes are juicier than European types. For flavor, Concord is outstanding and blue-black when fully matured. Popular also are the Delaware and Catawba varieties. Grapes should be well colored, plump, and firmly attached to the stem. White or green grapes are the sweetest when colored a yellowish cast or straw color, plus a tinge of amber. Red varieties are better when the good red predominates. Avoid soft, wrinkled, or leaky grapes. Once you have made your own raisins from grapes, you'll probably never want to buy commercial ones again, which are often preblanched and treated with chemicals, detracting from the genuine flavor of home-dried raisins.

Halves. Wash any variety. Remove from stems. Cut in half. Seeds may or may not be removed (remember, the seeds contain the nutrients for the next generation and are good for you). Place, cut side up, on trays and dry 24 to 48 hours, depending on size and sweetness of grapes, until raisins are chewy but do not stick together when stored. The sweeter the grapes, the longer it will take for them to dry and become raisins. Raisins will always be a little sticky. They make excellent snacks, or may be used without being reconstituted in your favorite recipe.

To Reconstitute. Place ½ cup raisins in narrow high-walled container so that ½ cup warm or hot water will almost cover them. Soak in refrigerator or at room temperature 1 or 2 hours or refrigerate overnight, until soft. Yield: ½ cup plus 1½ tablespoons of soft raisins.

Whole. Raisins have a nonporous skin which makes it difficult for moisture to be removed without blanching and breaking down the outside peel. Therefore, drying halves produces more flavorful, uncooked, unblanched, fresh flavor.

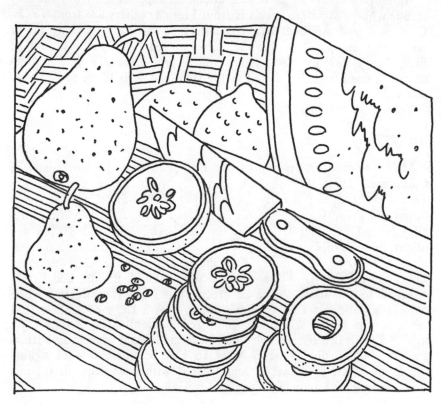

KUMQUATS

To dry, see "Oranges."

LEMONS

Available year round, most lemons come from California and Arizona. They should have a rich yellow color, be firm and heavy. Pale or greenish yellow ones have a slightly higher acidity. Coarse or rough skin is generally thick with less flesh content.
To dry, see "Oranges."

LIMES

Florida produces most of our green limes. The smaller yellow (Key) limes are usually imported. They should have a glossy skin and be heavy for their size.
To dry, see "Oranges."

MELONS

There are many varieties of melon: cantaloupe, casaba, crenshaw, honeyball, honeydew, Persian and watermelons. They dry beautifully, retaining their bright color. Selecting a good melon is difficult and can only be done with certainty by tasting it. Purchase one melon, take it home, and taste it; if it proves to be really good, buy more for drying.

Slices. Remove rind and seeds (the seeds may be washed and dried separately for growing more melons). Cut in ¼-inch slices and arrange on trays. Dry 12 to 18 hours or until leathery. Melon slices may be dipped in lemon before drying to cut the sweetness. They taste much sweeter when dried, and can be used as snacks or reconstituted and mixed with other fruit such as citrus, which combines well with the sweetness of melon. See Fruit Compote in Index.

To Reconstitute. Pour 1 cup water over 1 cup slices of dried melon. Soak 1 or 2 hours or refrigerate overnight. Add fresh lemon juice to taste.

Chunks. Watermelon dries best when cut in ½-inch chunks. Arrange on trays; dry about 24 hours, until almost hard but leathery. To reconstitute, see Slices. A little fresh lemon juice added to melon enhances the flavor.

ORANGES

When selecting oranges, avoid the very shiny, beautiful-appearing ones. Usually these are stamped with a national brand and have been waxed and embalmed with a biphenol chemical. A well-known friend who is a doctor said that he and his wife both began to notice a miserable itch after peeling and eating oranges. He went back to the store from which the oranges were purchased to see the shipping boxes which were stamped, "This product has been treated with biphenol to maintain its freshness." He noticed there was a chemical smell in the crates which had permeated the fruit—the peel for sure (who can be certain how far into the fruit the chemical went). The girl who was juicing the oranges told him, "If I don't wear gloves, my hands begin to blister and swell!"

How many food editors have printed recipes using grated orange rind not realizing this? I myself have developed many recipes using orange peel not knowing that I should state that the peel must come from organically grown oranges. I remember well the day I told this story to the company auditor who worked for this very same orange company. Though dubious, he could easily check to see if they indeed purchased any such chemical. He later informed me that not only was I incorrect but that his company was quite active in campaigning against the artificial coloring added to oranges. He added that the company he worked for did wax oranges, however, and that the wax contained chemicals to preserve them. He evidently was not aware that biphenol is one of the chemicals used in this preserving. So for health's sake, select organically grown unwaxed fruit.

Oranges are supplied year round from California, Florida, Texas, and Arizona. The California and Arizona leading varieties, Navel and Valencia, are both characterized by peel that is a rich orange color. The Navel orange, available from November until May, has a thicker, more pebbled skin than the Valencia, is easier to peel, and the segments separate readily making an ideal eating orange or for use in salads. Available from late April through October, the Valencia is excellent for juice or for slicing into salads. Florida and Texas crops are available from October until the end of June. Skin color is not a reliable indication of quality. Often fully matured fruit will turn greenish ("regreening") late in the marketing season. "Russeting," a tan, brown, or blackish mottling or speckling over the skin is often found on Florida and Texas oranges, but not on California varieties. It has no effect on eating quality, and often occurs on oranges with thin skin and superior eating quality. Select firm, heavy oranges with fresh, bright, reasonably smooth skin. Lightweight oranges lack flesh and juice. Rough oranges are thick-skinned.

Peel. Wash orange. Using vegetable peeler, peel round and round, removing outer colored part of peel from the white. Dry until hard, about 4 to 6 hours. Puree in blender to use for powdered or grated orange peel.

Cross-Cut Slices. Slice whole orange, peel and all, ¼ inch thick across fruit. Dry 12 to 24 hours or until hard. When eaten, fruit should not contain any pockets of liquid. The peel, which is normally bitter, will be much sweeter making the whole slice, peel and all, a snack which will please some, but not everybody.

To make orange juice, remove center of slice and puree in blender with water. Use ½ cup dried orange to 1 cup water.

Pieces. Cut away rind and white of fruit. Slice into ¼-inch-thick slices. then in wedges or pieces. Dry 12 to 24 hours or until hard and free from pockets of liquid. Delicious as a snack or may be pureed in blender with water for juice.

To Reconstitute. Soak ½ cup fruit in ½ cup water 1 or 2 hours or overnight until soft.

PAPAYA

Papaya retains bright color and fresh flavor when dried.

Slices. Cut in half, remove seeds. Arrange slices on trays; dry 8 to 12 hours, until brittle. Papaya slices may be dipped in lemon before drying, since it is normally served with lemon or lime juice. It can be reconstituted with lemon or lime juice added.

To Reconstitute. Use same procedure as for melons.

PEACHES AND NECTARINES

Peaches are of two general types: Freestone (flesh readily separates from the pit) and Clingstone (flesh clings tightly to the pit). Do not attempt to remove pit from Clingstone but cut thin slices away from pit. Peaches should be fairly firm but a trifle soft to the touch. The skin color between red areas should be yellow or creamy, not green. Avoid firm or hard peaches or overripe, very soft ones with bruises.

Nectarines combine the characteristics of both the peach and plum and are available from California from June through September. Rich color, plumpness, and a slight softening along the "seam" of the nectarine are desirable.

Slices. Wash. Cut into ¼-inch-thick slices, with or without peel. Arrange in single layers on tray. Dry 8 to 12 hours, depending on sweetness of fruit, until it is between a brittle and bendable state. Slices make excellent snacks or may be added, without being reconstituted to cereals, pancakes, waffles, cookies, and stuffing.

To Reconstitute. Use same procedure as for apricot slices.

PEARS

Bartlett, the most popular variety, available from August through November, is produced in California, Washington, and Oregon. Anjou, Bosc, Winter Nellis, and Comice can be found from November until May. Pears should be firm but beginning to soften to the touch. Bartletts should be a pale yellow to rich yellow color; Anjou or Comice— light green to yellowish green; Bosc—greenish yellow to brownish yellow (the brown cast is caused by skin russeting, a characteristic of the Bosc pear); Winter Nellis —medium to light green. Avoid cold storage pears which may darken when dried. Look for organically grown pears so that you may enjoy the added nutrition of peel and seeds.

Slices. Wash pears. Slice with or without peel, ¼ inch thick. Arrange in single layer on trays. Dry 10 to 14 hours or until rather dry but chewy. Dry pear slices will bend without snapping. Sweeter pears require a longer drying time. May be used as snacks (instead of candy) or added without being reconstituted to cereals, pancakes, waffles, breads, cookies, cakes, and stuffing.

To Reconstitute. Place ½ cup pears in narrow, high-walled container so that ½ cup warm water will almost cover them. Soak in refrigerator or at room temperature 30 minutes to 2 hours, or refrigerate overnight, until soft. Eat as fresh. Yield: ½ cup plus 1½ tablespoons. To make pear sauce or butter, puree ½ cup pears in blender with ½ cup water. Yield: ½ cup.

Rings. Use an apple or pear corer to remove center core, leaving pear in one piece. Cut pear, with or without peel, in ¼-inch slices across pear, making round circles. Dry in single layers on trays about 10 to 14 hours or until dry but chewy.

Cross-Cut Slices. Organically grown pears are delicious with both the peel and core left intact. Slice pears ¼ inch thick across, leaving in core and seeds. Dry in single layers 10 to 14 hours. The seeds contain the nutrition for the next generation, so don't waste them. Delicious as snacks or puree in blender for pear sauce.

PERSIMMONS

The many varieties of persimmons range from soft to hard when ripe.

Slices. Wash. Do not peel. Cut across round or center or persimmon into ⅜-inch-thick slices using very sharp knife. Place in single layers on trays. Dry 14 to 18 hours, until hard but still bendable.

To Reconstitute. Place ½ cup persimmons in narrow, high-walled container so that ½ cup warm water will almost cover them. Soak in refrigerator or at room temperature 1 or 2 hours or refrigerate overnight until soft. Eat as fresh or puree in blender for use in recipes. Persimmons and water may be pureed in blender without soaking. Yield: ½ cup plus 1½ tablespoons.

Wedges. Wash. Do not peel. Cut in ½-inch-thick wedges. Place wedges either standing or flat on trays. Dry 16 to 20 hours or until hard but bendable.

To Reconstitute. Use same procedure as for slices.

Orange or Lemon Juice Dip. Due to sweetness of persimmons, dipping slices or wedges in orange or lemon juice adds tartness and variety. Dry slices 16 to 20 hours; wedges 18 to 24 hours.

PINEAPPLES

Pineapples, available year round, from Puerto Rico, Hawaii, and Mexico, are at peak supply in April and May. Look for mature ones evidenced by plump, glossy eyes or pips, firmness, a lively color, heavy for size. On a ripe pineapple, the "spike" or leaves can be pulled out easily from the top. Avoid soft bruised fruit.

Slices. Wash pineapple, twist off green top, and cut in half lengthwise. Cut each half in four wedges. Using a sharp knife, remove core from each wedge, about 1/3 inch down from top point. Next, run knife between bottom skin and fruit. Slice down on fruit at ¼-inch intervals, from where core was removed to pineapple peel on bottom. Place ¼-inch-thick slices on tray. Dry about 24 hours or more, until dry but chewy. Fruit will always be a little sticky but pieces should not stick together when dry. Fantastic instead of candy! May be added without being reconstituted to cereals, pancakes, breads, waffles, cookies, stuffing, and cakes.

To Reconstitute. Use same procedure as for grapes.

PLUMS

Plums produced mostly in California are available June to September. Varieties and color vary greatly. Taste to be certain it appeals to you. Plums should have a good, deep color according to the type and be slightly firm to fairly soft in ripeness.

Slices. Do not peel. Wash and cut into ¼-inch-thick slices. Arrange in single layers on trays. Dry 8 to 10 hours, until fairly hard but chewable. Use sweet plum slices as snacks, or add to cereal and nuts.

To Reconstitute. Place ½ cup slices in narrow, high-walled container so that ½ cup warm water will almost cover them. Soak in refrigerator or at room temperature 1 or 2 hours or refrigerate overnight until soft. Eat as fresh or puree for sauce. Mixture can be pureed in blender for sauce without soaking.

Halves. Do not peel. Wash and cut into halves. Arrange in single layers on trays. Dry 36 to 40 hours, or until fairly hard but chewable. Use as snacks and add to cereal, nuts.

To Reconstitute. Use same procedure as for slices.

POMEGRANATES

Pomegranates are available around Thanksgiving and Christmas.

Seeds. Cut pomegranate in half. Pull away peel and remove seeds from membrane. Seeds are excellent pureed in blender for making fruit leather.

To Reconstitute. Tear Pomegranate Leather into pieces; puree ½ cup pieces with 1/3 cup or more water in blender to make sauce for ice cream or pudding.

RHUBARB

Mostly available from January to June, rhubarb is a highly distinctive vegetable used like a fruit in sweet sauces and pies. Stems should be fresh, firm, bright, and glossy.

Sliced. Cut in ½-inch slices. Dry about 18 to 20 hours, until hard.

To Reconstitute. Pour 1¼ cups hot water over 1 cup rhubarb and soak overnight. Yield: about 2 cups rhubarb for use in a pie or sauce.

Vegetables

ASPARAGUS

Although it is available from mid-February through June, the peak supply of asparagus is from April to mid-June. Tips should be compact and closed, with smooth round spears, and a fresh appearance. A rich green color covering most of the spear designates the tender part of the asparagus. The most usable tender part is easily selected by breaking it away from the lower part which won't break when bent.

Pieces. Wash, blot dry, and cut in ½-inch pieces. Place on tray; dry about 9 hours or until hard.

To Reconstitute. Pour 1½ cups hot water over 1 cup dried asparagus pieces in a narrow, high-walled container and let soak 1 to 2 hours, or refrigerate overnight, until soft, adding more water if needed. Yield: about 1½ cups. Cook by your usual method.

To Powder. Place very dry asparagus slices or dried broken spears in blender. Blend until powdered. Use in broth for soup, or for Cream of Asparagus Soup.

Whole Spears. Wash and blot dry. Place on tray. Dry thin spears approximately 15 hours, medium about 18 hours, and thick about 20 hours. To check dryness, and to reconstitute, follow same procedure as for pieces. Sticks may also be broken and powdered, using the same procedure as for pieces.

BEANS, SNAP

Beans are available throughout the year and should have a fresh, bright green color. Best are tender beans in firm, crisp pods.

Slices. For quickest drying, slice beans lengthwise and then across in ½- to 1-inch pieces. Place on trays and dry 5 to 7 hours, until hard. If not sliced lengthwise, they require 7 to 9 hours to dry.

To Reconstitute. Pour 2 cups hot water over 1 cup dried green beans. Let soak overnight. Yield: about 1¾ cups beans. Cook by usual method. Many prefer to blanch beans 5 minutes before drying, as it hastens reconstitution. Drying blanched green beans requires about 12 hours.

To Powder. Blend very dry green beans in blender until powdered. Use in soups or sauces.

BEETS

Available year round, beets should be firm, round, and have slender tap roots. The large main root should be a rich, deep red color with a smooth surface.

Slices. For slicing and drying beets, follow same procedure as for cauliflower. Dried beet slices may be eaten as a snack. They may be dried to a crisp chip if sliced ⅛ inch thick and dried for 6 or 7 hours.

To Reconstitute. Pour ¾ cup hot water over ¼ cup beets. Let soak 1 or 2 hours or overnight. Yield: about 1¼ cups. Cook by usual method.

Grated. Remove leaves from beets, wash, blot dry, and grate onto tray. Dry about 3 hours, until hard and slightly spongy.

To Reconstitute. Pour ¼ cup hot water over ¼ cup grated beets. Let soak 10 to 20 minutes. Yield: about ½ cup of fresh-tasting beets which are excellent when added to a salad or cooked in your usual way.

BEET TOPS

Follow procedure for Greens.

BROCCOLI

Available throughout the year, broccoli is least abundant in July and August. Look for firm, compact clusters of small flower buds which are dark or sage green in color. Avoid spread clusters with enlarged or open buds, yellowish green in color or wilted.

Quartered. Wash broccoli, blot dry, and cut into quarters lengthwise. Place on trays. Dry 6 to 10 hours, until hard but slightly spongy.

To Reconstitute. Cover stalks with hot water in a shallow pan. Let soak overnight. Cook by usual method. Many prefer to blanch stalks for 5 minutes before drying as it hastens reconstitution. Drying broccoli which has been blanched requires 12 to 14 hours.

To Powder. Place very dry broken pieces of broccoli in blender. Blend until powdered. Use in soups or sauces.

BRUSSELS SPROUTS

A close relative of cabbage, brussels sprouts are available about 10 months of the year, but are in peak supply from October through December. Look for fresh, bright green color, tight-fitting outer leaves, firm body, and freedom from blemishes.

Break apart brussels sprouts and proceed as in drying cabbage. Sprouts may be shredded, cut in squares or pieces, or left in fairly loose leaves. If broken apart into loose leaves, allow 6 to 10 hours to dry.

CABBAGE

Cabbage sold fresh is called "new" cabbage, or "old" cabbage if from storage. New cabbage can be purchased year round. In winter it comes mainly from California, Florida, and Texas. Many northern states grow cabbage for late summer and fall and hold in storage for winter use. Select new cabbage with dark leaves. If leaves have turned pale or white, it has not only lost color but most of its flavor and nutrition as well. Cold storage cabbage is usually trimmed of all outer leaves and lacks green color. Smooth-leaved green cabbage, crinkly-leaved green Savoy cabbage, and red cabbage make up three major groups of cabbage varieties. Look for good color with firm heads heavy for their size.

Shredded. Wash cabbage, remove core, shred, and spread evenly on trays so that cabbage is about ⅝ inch thick. Dry 4 to 6 hours, until crisp but still chewable. Delicious as a snack; reconstitute for cole slaw; add to soups or stews.

To Reconstitute. Pour ½ cup hot water over ½ cup shredded cabbage in a high-walled container so that water almost covers cabbage. Soak for about 10 minutes. Cool in its own liquid or chill for a salad. Yield: about ¾ cup cabbage crispy enough for salad or cole slaw.

Squares or Pieces. Cut washed cabbage in ½- to ¾-inch pieces. Spread on trays so that cabbage is about ⅝ inch thick. Dry 6 to 8 hours, until almost crispy but still chewable. Use as a snack or in soups, stews, and vegetable mixes, or reconstitute and cook in your usual way. To reconstitute, use same procedure as for shredded cabbage.

CARROTS

Carrots which are very high in calcium, phosphorous, vitamins and minerals are available year round with the majority coming from California and Texas. Firm, well-formed, smooth, well-colored carrots are most desirable.

Grated. Wash and grate carrots. Arrange evenly on trays so that carrots are ⅝ inch thick. Dry about 4 to 6 hours, until dry and almost hard. Carrots will appear lighter, but will reconstitute beautifully.

To Reconstitute. Pour 3 tablespoons warm water over 2 tablespoons grated carrots in a high-walled container. In 5 or 10 minutes, carrots will be fresh enough to add to a green salad. Yield: about 3½ tablespoons carrots. In larger amounts, ¾ cup carrots reconstituted in ½ cup water equals ⅞ cup. 1½ cups carrots reconstituted in 1 cup water equals 1¾ cups. Cook by your usual method in liquid in which carrots were reconstituted, adding water as needed. Chill if using in a salad.

Slices. Wash carrots, slice ¼ inch thick. Dry in a single layer on trays 6 to 8 hours until hard. Carrots will be lighter in color, but will reconstitute to original color.

To Reconstitute. Pour ½ cup water over ½ cup sliced dried carrots in a high-walled container. In 15 to 20 minutes, carrots will be fresh enough for a salad or to be eaten like fresh. Yield: about ⅞ to 1 cup carrot slices.

CAULIFLOWER

Cauliflower is most abundant from September through January but is available year round. The white edible portion (curd) should be white to creamy-white, compact, solid and clean. If leaves are still attached to head and are a good green color, the cauliflower is fresh.

Slices. Remove leaves, wash, blot dry, and break into flowerettes. Cut flowerettes into ¼-inch slices. Arrange in single layer on trays. Dry about 9 hours, until rather hard but still spongy. Can be eaten as a snack or served with a dip.

To Reconstitute. Pour 1½ cup hot water over ½ cup dried cauliflower in a narrow, high-walled container. Soak 1 or 2 hours, or refrigerate overnight, until soft, adding more water if needed. Yield: about 1¼ cups. Cook by usual method.

CELERY

Available throughout the year, celery is popular for a great many uses. It should be fresh and crisp with a solid, rigid feel. The surface should be slightly glossy and the color light green or medium green. Wilted celery with flabby upper branches or leaf stems, as well as pithy, hollow, or discolored centers in the branches, is not desirable.

Slices. Cut slices across stalks ¼ to ½ inch thick. Place in single layers on trays. Dry 6 to 10 hours, until hard and dry. Celery will be about 1/10 of its original size. The leaves may also be dried for use in soups, stews, and salads. Dry until they break when bent. Celery will appear dull in color but will return to original color when reconstituted. Pieces of dried celery or leaves may be added directly to soups, stews, casseroles, chili, and spaghetti sauce; they will reconstitute in the liquid. Dried leaves are a flavorful addition to salads.

To Reconstitute. Dried slices may be sauteed briefly in oil or unsalted butter for use in cooking. To reconstitute in water, pour 2 tablespoons of water over 2 tablespoons dried celery in a high-walled container. Soak 20 to 30 minutes. Yield: approximately 2½ to 3½ tablespoons celery.

CHINESE CABBAGE

Some varieties of Chinese Cabbage have a firm head and others an open, leafy form. They should be elongated and fresh, crisp, green plants without decay and blemishes. Wilted or yellowed plants are not desirable.

Dry Chinese Cabbage just like cabbage. Since it is primarily a salad vegetable, it can be added in the dried state to salads or reconstituted and chilled for a salad or use in Chinese cooking.

CORN

Sweet corn is most plentiful from early May until mid-September, although it can be found year round in many areas. Both yellow-kernel and white corn are sold. Fresh corn has husks with a good green color and silk-ends free from decay and worms. Ears should be well covered with plump, not-too-mature kernels. Very large, dark yellow kernels with depressed areas on the outer surface are old and overmature. Many believe that corn should be blanched before drying. However, this

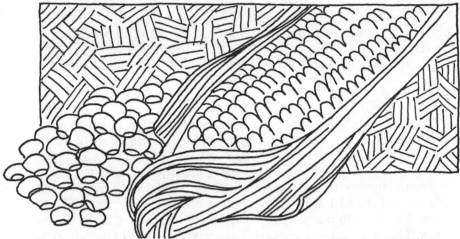

turns good nutrients into starch, and I have found it to be totally un-necessary and a waste of precious time and energy as well. Corn is very nutritious until we overcook it. For this reason, I developed the recipes for Fresh Corn Chips and Corn Tomato Chips made from fresh corn, dried in the dehydrator at the low temperature of 118 degrees. Even when serving corn on the cob, I bring water to a boil, turn off the heat, add the corn, cover, and let set for 3 minutes before eating. (It is never actually cooked).

Kernels. Cut kernels from cob and arrange in layers 2 or 3 kernels thick on tray. Dry 6 to 10 hours, until crispy. The sweeter the corn, the better it tastes, but the longer the drying process. Corn kernels will be dry, brittle, and break when mashed.

To Make Cornmeal. Dried corn may be ground in grinder or blender for use as cornmeal, or added to soups and stews.

To Reconstitute. Pour ½ cup hot water over ½ cup dried corn in a high-walled container. Soak 30 minutes to 2 hours or overnight, adding more water if necessary. Yield: about ⅝ to ¾ cup corn. Heat and cook in your usual manner.

Scraped. Prepare tray by spreading plastic wrap or parchment paper lengthwise on tray and taping each corner with transparent or masking tape to hold and stretch in place. Scrape creamy part of corn from which kernels of corn have already been cut, onto lined trays. Scraped creamy appearing corn should be ⅛ to ¼ inch thick and can be spread with a rubber scraper into a 9 by 13 inch rectangle as for Fresh Corn Chips or Corn Tomato Chips. Dry 8 to 10 hours until crisp, brittle, easy to

break into chips, and partially pulls away from liner while still in dehydrator. Corn will crinkle and bulge on tray in an attractive manner.
Break into corn chips to eat or reconstitute by the same procedure as
for kernels. To make Cream Style Corn, add half and half, butter, pepper,
honey, and thicken slightly with freshly ground whole wheat flour.

CUCUMBERS

Cucumbers are in abundance during summer months, although available year round. Check for good green color and firmness over entire
area. They should be well shaped and developed, but not over 2½ inches
in diameter. Overmature cucumbers which are larger in diameter, have a
dull color turning toward yellow, have withered and shriveled ends,
and are tough and bitter tasting. Young desirable cucumbers may be
greenish-white with many small bumps on the surface. Cucumbers are
almost always waxed as a preserving process, especially in the winter or
less productive seasons. You can feel the greasy texture by touching.
They may not be waxed in summer. Although peel is nutritious and good
to eat, peel cucumbers if they have been waxed or they will become
bitter tasting when dried.

Slices. Wash and dry cucumbers. Peel if waxed. If not waxed, dry with
or without peel, as desired. Cut into ⅛- to ¼-inch-thick slices. Arrange
in a single layer on dehydrator trays. Slices may be placed next to each
other, touching, but not overlapping. Dry 6 to 10 hours, depending on
thickness of slices and moisture in the air. Cucumbers should be crisp,
snap when broken, and rattle if stored in a bag or glass jar. The
natural salt in cucumber slices is more concentrated when dried, so the
dried slices taste almost as if they had been salted and make a tasty and
nutritious snack instead of potato chips. They are delightful when added
to a salad without reconstituting. Dried cucumbers may be powdered in
blender for use in a soup or sauce.

To Reconstitute. Pour ½ cup very warm water over ½ cup dried cucumbers in a high-walled container so that water almost covers them. Soak
10 to 20 minutes. Yield: about ½ cup plus 1½ tablespoons. Chill for use
in a salad. Dried cucumbers (½ cup) may also be reconstituted in
¼ cup vinegar and ¼ cup oil along with a little freshly chopped or dried
onion and herbs to taste. Cucumber will have a fresh lovely flavor, but
will be limp. Just as a raisin never returns to a grape but is delicious
in its own right, so is a dried cucumber. It never returns to a crisp slice
but is flavorful and appetizing. To powder: puree very dry cucumbers
in blender until powdered. Use in sauces, salads, or soups, such as
Chilled Cucumber Soup.

EGGPLANT

Although most plentiful during late summer, eggplant can be found to some extent year round. It should be firm, smooth, heavy, and dark purple. Do not purchase if it is soft, shriveled, cut, poorly colored, or with irregular dark brown spots (signs of decay).

Slices. Wash and dry eggplant. Eggplant may be dried with or without peel as desired. Cut into ¼- to ½-inch slices. Arrange in a single layer on trays, touching but not overlapping. Dry 8 to 16 hours, depending on thickness of slices and moisture in the air. Eggplant should be spongy, leathery, and dry—almost hard.

To Reconstitute. Pour 1 cup hot water over 1 cup eggplant in a narrow, high-walled container. Soak 1 or 2 hours, or refrigerate overnight, until soft. Yield: about 1 1/3 cups. Cook by usual method.

Cubes. Cut eggplant into ¼- to ½-inch cubes (with or without peel). Place in single layer on trays. Dry 6 to 14 hours, until spongy, leathery, and dry—almost hard. To reconstitute, use same procedure as for slices.

GARLIC

Follow same procedure as for Onions.

GREENS

Greens include a large number of widely differing species of plants: endive, escarole, kale, collards, turnip tops, beet tops, chard, mustard greens, broccoli leaves, chicory, dandelion greens, watercress, and sorrel. Follow same procedure as for spinach.

MUSHROOMS

Mushrooms are grown in houses, cellars, or caves and are available year round. Most desirable are young, small to medium size mushrooms. Caps (the wide portion on top) should either be closed or moderately open with pink or light-tan gills (rows of paper-thin tissue underneath the cap). The cap should be white, creamy, or light brown. Avoid overripe, wide open caps, and dark gills.

Whole. Wash and blot dry mushrooms. Small ones may be dried whole, including stem. Arrange in single layer on tray. Dry 5 to 7 hours, until spongy and leathery. Dried mushrooms may be added directly to stews, soups, vegetables, and sauces. They will reconstitute in cooking.

To Reconstitute. Pour ¼ cup hot water over ¼ cup dried mushrooms in narrow, high-walled container. Soak 20 to 30 minutes or longer, until soft, adding more water if needed. Yield: about 1/3 cup mushrooms. Cook by usual method.

Slices. Cut clean, dry mushrooms in ¼-inch-thick slices. Place on trays. Dry about 3 or 4 hours. To check dryness and reconstitute, use same procedure as for whole mushrooms.

ONIONS

Available year round, onions come in many varieties in shades of white, yellow, and purple. They should be firm or hard, dry, with small necks, covered with papery outer scales, free from green sunburn spots and blemishes. Do not select onions with wet or very soft necks which reveal immaturity or decay. Avoid those with thick, hollow, woody centers or with fresh sprouts.

Cross-Cut Slices or Rings. Remove papery outer scales. Wash, dry, and cut across into ⅛- to ¼-inch slices. Arrange in single layers on trays, although slices may overlap to some degree. Dry 8 to 12 hours, until dry but bendable. Slices may be dried until they break when bent, for long-term storage or for powdering in blender for onion powder. Sliced, dried onion may be added, without being reconstituted, to salads, stews, soups, vegetables, spaghetti sauce, etc.

To Reconstitute. Follow same procedure as for reconstituting celery; ½ cup hot water poured over ½ cup onions yields about 2/3 cup.

To Powder. Place very dry sliced or chopped dried onion in blender. Blend until powdered. Use dried onion powder as seasoning.

Chopped. Follow same procedure as for Peppers.

ONIONS: GREEN, SHALLOTS, LEEKS

Follow same procedure as for Onions.

PARSLEY

Parsley, available year round, ranks at the top of vegetables with vitamin A. It should be fresh, crisp, and have bright green leaves.

Sprigs. Wash, blot dry, and cut into small sprigs. Place in single layers on trays. Dry 2½ to 3½ hours, until dry and breakable. Store in glass jars to prevent crushing. Cut, snip, or crumble into small pieces for use in salads, vegetables, and meats.

PEAS

Peas should be young, a beautiful light green, tender and sweet.

Shelled. Place shelled peas in single layer on trays. Dry 14 to 16 hours, until hard and dry. 1½ cups fresh peas will yield about 1/3 cup plus 1 tablespoon dried.

To Powder. Peas may be powdered in blender for making A Cup Of Soup (Split Pea). 3 tablespoons dried peas pureed in blender will yield about 3 tablespoons of powder for putting in soup or broth.

To Reconstitute. Pour 1 cup hot water over ½ cup peas in a high-walled container. Soak overnight (8 to 12 hours), until soft. Cook in liquid, adding more water if needed, until tender. Season with un-salted butter and pepper as desired. Yield: about 1¼ cups peas. 4 or 5 servings.

PEPPERS

Sweet green peppers, although available throughout the year, are most plentiful during the late summer months. They should have firm walls, relatively heavy weight, medium to dark green color, and a glossy sheen. Avoid thin walled, lightweight, flimsy, wilted, or flabby peppers with cuts or punctures. Soft, watery spots on the sides are evidence of decay. It is best to buy peppers for drying in season, directly from the farm, or grow them since many are waxed for pre-serving and appearance. Waxed surfaces become concentrated and bitter when dried, so it is best to avoid them. Hot peppers and other varieties used in Mexican foods are not generally waxed and can be dried like sweet green peppers.

Slices, Strips, or Cross-Cut Rings. Cut in ¼-inch-thick slices or lengthwise strips. Wash, dry, and cut peppers in half lengthwise, discarding seeds. For cross-cut slices, cut into ¼-inch thick slices across pepper. Arrange in single layers on trays, although slices may overlap to some degree. Dry 6 to 8 hours, until dry but bendable. For long-term storage, slices may be dried until they break when bent.

Sliced dried green pepper can be added, without being reconstituted, to salads, soups, stews, vegetables, spaghetti sauce. Some people enjoy them as a snack.

To Reconstitute. Pour 2 tablespoons warm or hot water over 2 tablespoons dried green pepper in a narrow, high-walled container. Soak 20 to 30 minutes. Yield: approximately 2½ tablespoons.

To Powder. Place very dry slices of pepper in blender. Blend until powdered. Use as seasoning and in soups.

Chopped. Cut pepper into medium-sized or coarse pieces. Place on trays and dry 5 to 8 hours. To check dryness and reconstitute, follow same procedure for slices, strips, or cross-cut rings. Medium-size pieces of green pepper require approximately 10 to 20 minutes to reconstitute in water.

POTATOES

Potatoes available year round, come in many varieties, although they fit into three general categories: new, general purpose, and baking potatoes. How potatoes can be dried depends on geographical location, amount of moisture in soil, if held in cold storage, and other factors.

Slices. Wash and cut potatoes (with or without peel) into ¼-inch thick squares or slices. Soak 30 minutes to 1 hour in ½ gallon water to which ½ cup lemon juice has been added. Drain in colander and arrange on trays. Dry 8 to 10 hours or until hard and dry. Many believe steaming potatoes for 5 minutes helps to retain whiteness. Arrange on trays. Dry 10 to 12 hours.

To Reconstitute. Pour 1 cup hot water over 1 cup dried potatoes. Soak 2 hours or overnight. Yield: about 1 1/3 cups. Cook by usual method.

Grated. Follow same drying procedure as for slices. Dry 5 to 7 hours. To reconstitute, follow same procedure as for slices.

Mashed. Wash, peel, and cook potatoes. Mash, adding potato water or milk, until potatoes are consistency of fruit leather. Spread plastic wrap or parchment paper lengthwise over tray and tape each corner to tray with transparent or masking tape. Using 1½ to 2 cups potato mixture per tray, spread mixture ¼ inch thick using rubber scraper. Dry 8 to 12 hours, until mixture is hard and can be pulled off wrap. Usually, after 6 to 8 hours, potatoes can be pulled off wrap and dried directly on tray. For mashed, powder dried potatoes in blender and whip together 1¾ to 2 cups hot milk and cream, 3 tablespoons melted butter, and 1 cup dried powdered potato. Yield: about 1¾ to 2 cups.

PUMPKIN

Pumpkins are available from September until the end of January.

Slices or Mashed. Wash and peel. Dry and reconstitute following the same procedure as for Winter Squash. Powdered pumpkin is excellent in ice cream.

Pumpkin Seeds. Wash and place in single layer on trays. Dry about 5 hours until dry; they should rattle in a glass or plastic container. They make a wonderful snack or may be ground and used in breads, cookies, and drinks.

RADISHES

Available year round, radishes are most plentiful from May through July. They should be plump, round, firm and of a good red color.
Use same procedure as for Beets for slicing, grating, drying, and reconstituting. Add radishes to salads; do not cook.

SPINACH

Spinach should be a beautiful deep green with small to medium leaves. Stems or stalks should be young and tender, not coarse, large and tough.

Squares or Pieces. Cut washed, dried, spinach into ½- to ¾-inch pieces. Spread in one or two layers on trays. Dry 3 to 6 hours, until crisp. Leaves will be very fragile. Store in a glass container to prevent them from being crushed. When crushed it's delightful over salad.

To Powder. Puree in blender for Spinach Soup or Spinach Noodles.

To Reconstitute. Place 1½ cups leafy dried spinach in a colander; run hot water through it. Add unsalted butter, pepper, and seasoning. Yield: about ½ cup or 2 servings spinach.

SPROUTS

Most varieties of sprouts (alfalfa, mung bean, wheat and rye sprouts) dry beautifully to sprinkle over salads or eat as snacks. Place on trays and dry 2½ to 8 hours, depending on variety of sprout.

To Reconstitute. Pour 1 cup hot water over ½ cup sprouts. Soak 10 minutes. Chill to serve. Yield: about 2/3 cup sprouts.

SQUASH (SUMMER)

The yellow Crookneck, the large yellow Straightneck, the greenish-white Patty Pan, the slender green Zucchini, and the Italian Marrow are summer squash which are harvested while still immature, tender and edible. Normally, they are not waxed, as are cucumbers, so the "peel" is quite edible. Squash should be well-developed, as well as firm, fresh-looking, and well-formed. Skin should be glossy instead of dull, not hard or tough. Overmature or old squash has a dull appearance and a hard, tough surface with enlarged seeds and dry, stringy flesh.

Grating. Summer squash may be washed and grated. Zucchini is especially good when grated and made into Zucchini Bread. Arrange evenly in rectangular shape on shelves, in layers ⅜ to ¼ inch thick. Dry 10 to 12 hours, until easy to pull away from trays. Break into pieces for storage or to be powdered in blender.

To Reconstitute. Pour ½ cup hot water over ½ cup grated squash. Soak about 20 to 30 minutes. Yield: about ½ cup.

Slices. Wash and cut into ⅛- to ¼-inch slices. Dry in single layers on trays about 6 to 8 hours, until crisp and hard. When properly dried, zucchini slices will rattle in a bag or container. Great as a snack instead of potato chips. Serve as chip with a dip, or add, unreconstituted to salads, soups and stews.

To Reconstitute. Follow same procedure as for grated squash. Soak 15 to 30 minutes. Yield: ½ cup plus 1½ tablespoons squash.

SQUASH (WINTER)

Acorn (available year round), Butternut, Buttercup, green and blue Hubbard, green and gold Delicious, and Barbara (available from beginning of fall through winter) are marketed only when fully mature. They should be mature with a hard, tough rind. If heavy for their size, there will be a thick wall, and more flesh for eating. A tender rind indicates immaturity and poor quality.

Slices. Wash and peel squash. Follow the same procedure as for summer squash for drying and reconstituting. (Soaking ½ cup squash in ½ cup hot water 15 to 30 minutes will yield ½ cup plus 1½ tablespoons acorn squash or about 1 cup if banana squash.)

Mashed Squash. Remove rind and cut squash into chunks. Add water and cook, covered, until tender. Mash, using potato masher or beater. Line tray with plastic wrap or parchment paper and tape each corner to tray with transparent or masking tape. Spread ¼-inch thick. Dry about 4 to 6 hours, until dry, crisp, and hard.

To Reconstitute. Place in blender; add ¾ to 1 cup hot water to 1 cup powder, and blend until of desired consistency, adding more water as needed. Add seasonings and butter to taste. Heat through in saucepan or in oven in casserole dish.

SWEET POTATOES

Two types of sweet potatoes are available year round. Yams, the most common, have an orange color flesh and are very sweet. The regular sweet potato is a lighter, more yellow color.

Slices and Grated. Follow same procedure as for potatoes to dry and reconstitute.

Mashed. Wash, peel, and cook potatoes. Mash, adding potato water, or half orange and half pineapple juice, until potatoes are the consistency of fruit leather. Spread plastic wrap or parchment paper lengthwise over tray and tape to tray with transparent or masking tape. Using 1½ to 2 cups potato mixture per tray, spread mixture ¼ inch thick. Dry 12 to 16 hours until leathery but not hard.

To Reconstitute Mashed Potatoes. Pour 1 cup hot water over 1 cup dried mashed sweet potatoes. Soak 30 minutes to 1 hour or overnight. Season to taste, heat, and serve. Yield: about 1 cup.

TOMATOES

Tomatoes, available year round, are plentiful during September. "Home grown" or those purchased from nearby farms have the best flavor and most nutrition, since they are allowed to ripen completely before picked. Fully ripe, it will have an overall rich red color and a slight softness easy to detect by gentle handling.

Slices. My favorite method for drying tomatoes is to slice them ¼ inch thick with peel left on (it's easier and tomatoes remain firmer). However, tomatoes may be dried with or without the peel as desired.

Place a small cutting board inside a pizza or jelly-roll pan with ¾ inch sides to catch the juice as tomatoes are being sliced. A twenty-pound lug of tomatoes will yield 1 to 1½ cups of fresh wonderful juice as they are being sliced. Place tomato slices in single layers on tray, with sides touching but not overlapping. Some people fear that with a dehydrator full of tomatoes, a lot of juice will run to the bottom of the dehydrator, but if you use the kind of good quality dehydrator recommended and keep the temperature low (110 to 118 degrees) not more than 3 or 4 drops will appear on the bottom floor of the dehydrator and these may be easily wiped away with a sponge. (A high temperature dehydrator will cook the tomatoes, drawing out the juice.)

Place each tray of tomatoes in dehydrator as they are sliced. Dry approximately 12 hours, until crisp and brittle. Slices can be dried to the stage where they will still bend without breaking, or to an even dryer stage where they will break when bent, which is necessary for making tomato powder. Dried tomato slices or chips are excellent with a meal, as a snack, served with a dip. They can also be broken and added to salads, soups, stews, vegetables, or casseroles.

To Reconstitute. Place each dried tomato slice on a separate plate and sprinkle generously with water; saturate top of slice well but not so much that it floats in water. Let stand 10 to 20 minutes, refrigerated or at room temperature. Tomato slices will not return fully to their original size, but will taste very fresh, suitable for use in sandwiches or salads.

To Powder. Place very dry tomato slices in blender. Blend until completely powdered. If tomatoes stick together and do not powder, they are not dry enough and should be returned to the trays and dried until they powder easily. Five pounds of fresh tomatoes (16 cups sliced) will yield enough dried slices to make 1 cup dried powdered tomato or tomato powder. Use it in cooking and to make tomato paste, sauce, catsup, juice, soup.

Wedges. Cut tomatoes into ½-inch wedges, with or without peel. Place on tray with base of wedge on tray and triangular point up. Dry 16 to 20 hours. To check for dryness and reconstitution, follow same procedure as for Slices.

Chopped. Coarsely chop tomatoes with or without peel. Place on tray. Dry 10 to 14 hours. To check dryness, see slices.

Tempting Concoctions
To Make in Your Dryer

The recipes in this chapter have been specially prepared to help you make a host of delightful dishes in your dehydrator any time you wish. For best results, use only the recommended temperature range of 110 degrees to 118 degrees. Recipes referred to elsewhere in the book may be found in Index. Categories in this chapter are:

Beef	Cookies or Bars	Noodles
Breads	Crackers	Poultry
Cereals	Fish	Snacks
Cheeses	Jams	Soup
Complete Meals	Leathers	Yogurt
		Pet Food

BEEF

Beef Jerky (Not Marinated)

1¼ to 1½ pounds beef round steak, chuck, brisket, or flank steak
Freshly ground black pepper
Salt Substitute

Remove all gristle and fat from meat. Slice meat across grain in strips ⅛ to ¼ inch thick (for easier cutting, freeze meat and thaw enough to slice easily). Arrange meat in a single layer on dehydrator trays. Sprinkle as desired with pepper and Salt Substitute. Dry about 5 hours or overnight. Yield: about 6 ounces.

Favorite Beef Jerky

1¼ to 1½ pounds beef round steak, chuck, brisket or flank steak
¼ cup soy sauce
1 tablespoon Worcestershire Sauce
¼ teaspoon freshly ground pepper
⅛ to ¼ teaspoon dried powdered garlic
½ teaspoon dried powdered onion
⅛ teaspoon freshly grated nutmeg
⅛ to ¼ teaspoon ground ginger

Remove all gristle and fat from meat. Cut meat across the grain in strips ⅛ to ¼ inch thick (for easier cutting, freeze meat and thaw enough to slice easily). Mix together remaining ingredients and pour over meat. Distribute marinade well through meat. Refrigerate, covered, 5 hours or overnight. Arrange meat in a single layer on dehydrator trays. Dry about 5 hours, or overnight. Yield: about 6 ounces.

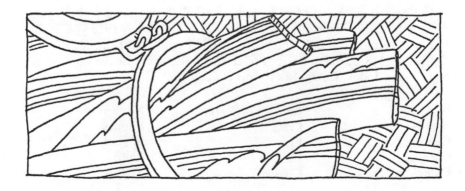

Beef Jerky with Chili

To the recipe for Favorite Beef Jerky: add to the marinade mixture 2 tablespoons chili sauce or catsup, and ⅛ to ¼ teaspoon liquid smoke before marinating.

Beef Jerky Sticks

> 1 pound very lean ground beef
> 3 tablespoons soy sauce
> 1 tablespoon Worcestershire sauce
> ¼ teaspoon freshly ground pepper
> ¼ teaspoon dried powdered onion
> ⅛ teaspoon dried powdered garlic
> ⅛ teaspoon freshly ground nutmeg
> ⅛ teaspoon ground ginger

Since all commercially ground beef contains some fat and fat will not dehydrate and turns rancid, it is best to select a lean piece of beef and grind it yourself or have the butcher grind it for you.

Mix all ingredients together thoroughly. Prepare one tray. Spread plastic wrap or parchment paper lengthwise over dehydrator tray, and tape each corner to tray with transparent or masking tape. Place mixture between two sheets of waxed paper and using rolling pin, roll mixture about ⅛ to ¼ inch thick into a 10-by-14 inch rectangular shape. Remove one sheet of waxed paper from meat. Place meat on lined tray, remove other sheet of waxed paper. Place tray in dehydrator. Dry 4 hours. Remove meat from tray, discard lining, and return meat to tray. Blot any excess fat with paper towel. Using kitchen shears, cut into ½-by-5-inch sticks. Continue to dry, blotting occasionally with paper towels, until meat is dry like jerky—about 5 more hours. Yield: 56 sticks.

Tasty Beef Cheese Sticks

> 1 pound very lean ground beef
> 1 cup grated Parmesan cheese
> 2 teaspoons dried powdered tomato
> 1 teaspoon freshly ground black pepper
> 1 teaspoon dried crushed basil
> 1 teaspoon dried powdered garlic
> ¼ teaspoon dried crushed oregano
> ¼ teaspoon dried crushed parsley

All commercially ground beef contains some fat. Fat will not dehydrate and turns rancid. Therefore, it is best to select a lean piece
of beef and grind it yourself or have the butcher grind it for you.

Mix all ingredients together thoroughly. Place mixture between
two sheets of waxed paper. Using rolling pin, roll about ⅛ to ¼ inch
thick into a rectangular shape about 10 by 14 inches. Spread plastic
wrap or parchment paper lengthwise over dehydrator tray and tape
each corner to tray with transparent or masking tape. Prepare one
tray. Remove one sheet of waxed paper from meat. Place meat directly on wrap or paper; remove other sheet of waxed paper. Place tray
in dehydrator and dry 4 hours. Remove meat from tray, discard lining
and return meat to tray. Blot any excess fat with paper towel. Using
kitchen shears, cut into ½-by-5-inch sticks. Continue to dry, blotting
occasionally with paper towels, until meat is dry like jerky—about 5
more hours. Yield: 56 sticks.

Tacos

    1 pound lean ground beef
    1 tablespoon apricot or soy oil
    1 small green pepper, chopped
    1 medium onion, finely chopped
    1 cup chopped fresh tomatoes or an 8-ounce can of tomatoes,
        chopped
    1 tablespoon chili powder
    1 teaspoon coriander
    ¾ to 1 cup water
    6 taco shells, heated
    1½ cups shredded lettuce
    ¾ cup grated cheddar cheese
    Hot sauce, if desired

Cook meat in oil until it changes color. Pour off drippings. Add
green pepper, onion, tomatoes, chili powder, and coriander. Simmer together a few minutes, stirring occasionally, to blend flavors
and cook vegetables. Prepare one tray. Spread plastic wrap or parchment paper lengthwise over dehydrator tray, and tape each corner
to tray with transparent or masking tape. Spread taco mixture ⅜ to ½
inch thick. Dry 6 to 8 hours, or until crumbly. Remove mixture from
liner and store. In this stage dried taco mix makes a delicious snack.

To reconstitute and make tacos: place dried taco mixture in heavy
pan with lid. Add ½ cup water and steam. Add ¼ to ½ cup more water
stirring and steaming until reconstituted and hot. In each taco shell,
spoon about one sixth of mixture, ¼ cup shredded lettuce and 2 tablespoons grated cheese. Serve with hot sauce. Yield: 6 servings.

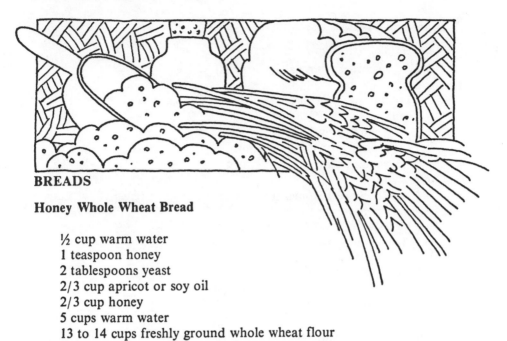

BREADS

Honey Whole Wheat Bread

½ cup warm water
1 teaspoon honey
2 tablespoons yeast
2/3 cup apricot or soy oil
2/3 cup honey
5 cups warm water
13 to 14 cups freshly ground whole wheat flour

Mix warm water and honey in metal container. Sprinkle with yeast. Set container holding yeast mixture in container of warm water to activate yeast. Let set 12 to 15 minutes or until yeast is bubbly.

While yeast is rising, combine in mixer oil, honey and warm water. Turn on bread mixer and add 7 cups flour. Mix thoroughly. Add yeast mixture and blend. Sprinkle in 3 to 4 cups flour while mixing 5 more minutes. Add another 3 cups flour. Mix an additional 5 minutes (add enough flour so that when you touch it with your hand, dough will not stick to it); dough will begin to pull away slightly from the side. Turn off mixer. Sprinkle plastic slab or board with flour. Cut and shape dough into four loaves. Place each into a greased 8½-by-4½-by-2½ inch pan. Remove 3 or 4 bottom shelves from dehydrator. Place loaves on bottom of dehydrator. Turn dehydrator on; let dough rise until doubled. Bake in oven 350 degrees for 30 minutes or until done. Yield: 4 one-pound loaves.

Use 1 pound of unbaked dough to make pizza, coffeecake or rolls. If you wish to use triticale (the hybrid cross between wheat and rye which is about 44% protein) in this recipe, substitute 3 cups triticale for 3 cups whole wheat flour. Total recipe may then require a little extra flour; 1½ cups freshly ground millet and 1½ cups freshly ground rye flour may also be substituted for 3 cups whole wheat flour in recipe. A little additional flour may also be needed when using part millet and rye flour.

Prune and Cheese Twist

Prune Filling
    1½ cups dried plum halves (prunes)
    1½ cups water
    1 pound Honey Whole Wheat Bread Dough (use ¼ of recipe)
    ¼ cup raisins
    ¼ cup chopped walnuts
    1 tablespoon grated orange rind
    ⅛ teaspoon freshly grated nutmeg
Cheese Filling
    1 cup (8 ounces) Homemade Cream Cheese, softened
    ¼ cup honey
    3 tablespoons grated orange rind
    1/3 cup white raisins
    1 egg, lightly beaten
    1½ teaspoons honey
    2 tablespoons finely chopped walnuts
    ¼ teaspoon grated orange rind

Soak prunes in water overnight. Puree prunes in blender and add enough of the liquid in which they were soaked to make ¾ cup of thick prune butter. Divide bread dough in half. On lightly floured board or waxed paper, roll each piece to a 10-by-12 inch rectangle.

For Prune Filling, mix together prune butter, raisins, walnuts, 1 tablespoon orange rind, and nutmeg. For Cheese Filling, mix together cream cheese, ¼ cup honey, 3 tablespoons orange rind, and raisins. Spread one rectangle with the Prune Filling. Spread the other rectangle with Cheese Filling. Roll up each from the 12-inch side like a jelly roll. Moisten edges with water and press to seal. Place rolls (seam side down) next to each other on a greased baking sheet. Pinch one end of rolls together. Twist around each other carefully without stretching and press ends to fasten. Brush with egg which has been mixed with honey. Sprinkle with walnuts and ¼ teaspoon grated orange rind. Remove three or four bottom shelves from dehydrator. Place Prune and Cheese Twist on bottom of dehydrator. Turn dehydrator on. Let rise until double. Bake in oven at 375 degrees for 20 to 25 minutes or until done. Cool on wire rack. Yield: 1 twist.

CEREALS

Granola

For the maximum nutritional value as well as fresher, more flavorful granola, make your own. Grind wheat and soy flour fresh. Make seven-grain cereal by combining and grinding equal parts of millet, buckwheat, brown rice, dried corn, wheat, barley, and rye. Use corn dried in your dehydrator. Raw nuts and seeds which have not been salted, processed, or heated to a high temperature give added food value. Chia seeds look like poppy seeds but are the tiny black seeds that Indians took along in a little pouch on hunting trips for nourishment. They are normally available in health food stores. By drying the granola at a low temperature 110 degrees to 118 degrees in the dehydrator, you'll retain as much nutrition as possible of the freshly whole grains, raw nuts, and seeds.

2 tablespoons chia seeds
½ cup water
¾ cup honey
3½ cups rolled oats
1½ cups wheat germ
1 cup freshly ground wheat flour
1 cup freshly ground soy flour
1 cup unsweetened coconut
½ cup seven-grain cereal (see above)
½ cup raw almonds
½ cup chopped walnuts
½ cup raw sunflower seeds
½ cup raw sesame seeds
2 tablespoons alfalfa seeds

Soak chia seeds overnight in ½ cup water. They will expand and thicken the water. Add honey. Mix well. In a 4-quart bowl, mix together all remaining ingredients. Pour honey-chia seed mixture over dry ingredients and mix well. Prepare five trays. Spread plastic wrap or parchment paper lengthwise over dehydrator tray, and tape each corner to tray with transparent or masking tape. Spread mixture ⅜ to ½ inch thick on trays. Dry 6 to 8 hours or overnight. Store in airtight containers in refrigerator. Yield: 11 cups.

Serve with milk and, if desired, sliced fresh fruit or any of the following or combination of dried fruits: apple, peach, pear, fig or persimmon slices, banana chips, raisins, prune halves, diced apricots or dates.

Health Cereal

     3 cups rolled oats
     1 cup wheat germ
     1 cup raw peanuts
     1 cup raw sesame seeds
     1 cup raw whole or chopped almonds
     1/3 cup honey
     ¼ cup water
     1 cup finely snipped dried apricots
     1 cup finely snipped dried apples
     1 cup finely snipped, pitted dried prunes

Mix together oats, wheat germ, peanuts, sesame seeds, and almonds in a large bowl. Blend honey and water. Pour over dry ingredients, mixing well. Stir in apricots, apples, and prunes. Prepare five trays. Spread plastic wrap or parchment paper lengthwise over each dehydrator tray, and tape each corner to the tray with transparent masking tape. Spread mixture ⅜ to ½ inch thick on trays. Place in dehydrator and dry 6 to 8 hours or overnight. Store in airtight containers in refrigerator. Yield: about 10 cups. Serve with milk.

CHEESES

Homemade Cottage Cheese

     2 quarts raw milk
     2½ tablespoons fresh lemon juice

Mix together raw milk and lemon juice and pour into two shallow glass or crockery (not metal) bowls. Remove the three bottom trays of dehydrator. Place bowls in bottom of dehydrator for 3 to 4 hours or until mixture begins to thicken. Line a large glass bowl with several layers of cheese cloth or a piece of old sheet which has been laundered many times. Pour raw milk mixture into lined bowl. Bring edges of cloth together and tie with cord. Elevate bag above bowl so whey will drip out. Let stand at room temperature overnight. Open bag and dip out fresh cottage cheese. Delicious as is or it may be seasoned. Store in refrigerator. Yield: about 1 cup.

Homemade Cream Cheese

Homemade Cream Cheese is heavenly, very easy to make, and costs about half as much as commercial varieties.

2 quarts buttermilk
2½ tablespoons fresh lemon juice

Mix together buttermilk and lemon juice and pour into two shallow glass or crockery (not metal) bowls. Remove the three bottom trays of dehydrator. Place bowls in bottom of dehydrator for 3 to 4 hours or until mixture begins to thicken. Line a large glass bowl with several layers of cheese cloth or a piece of old sheet which has been laundered many times. Pour buttermilk mixture into lined bowl. Bring edges of cloth together and tie with cord. Elevate bag above bowl so whey will drip out. Let stand at room temperature overnight. Open bag and dip out fresh cream cheese. Yield: about 1 cup. May be used as is or seasoned. Store in refrigerator.

COMPLETE MEALS

Chicken or Turkey Noodle Dinner

3 cups chicken or turkey broth (use 3 cups water plus 3 chicken
    bouillon cubes if broth is unavailable)
3 medium carrots, coarsely grated
3½ cups (8 ounces) Homemade Noodles (use half the recipe)
1 tablespoon dried crushed parsley
¾ teaspoon dried powdered onion
¼ to ½ teaspoon dried powdered sage
¼ teaspoon poultry seasoning
2½ tablespoons freshly ground whole-wheat flour
1½ cups cooked diced (½-inch cubes) chicken or turkey

Bring 2¾ cups broth or bouillon to a boil (reserve remaining ¼ cup for later use). Add carrots, noodles, parsley, onion, sage, and poultry seasoning. Simmer 10 to 15 minutes, stirring occasionally, until noodles and carrots are tender. Add remaining ¼ cup broth or bouillon slowly to flour, stirring to make a smooth paste. Add a little liquid from noodles to flour mixture, then stir flour mixture into noodles. Cook until slightly thickened. Stir in chicken or turkey. Cool. Prepare three trays. Spread plastic wrap or parchment paper length-wise over dehydrator tray, taping each corner to tray with transparent or masking tape. Spread 1½ to 2 cups noodle mixture on each tray, ¼ to ⅜-inch thick. Dry 10 to 12 hours or overnight. Peel noodle mixture off liner and discard liner, and continue drying 2 or 3 more hours. To reconstitute for an easy evening meal, in the morning place dried noodle mixture in 1½- or 2-quart casserole and pour 2½ cups cold water over it. Cover until evening. Heat over a *very low* heat, stirring occasionally, until mixture is thoroughly heated. There is no need to boil, as flavors are already blended. Serves 2.

Corned Beef and Rice

>   4 cups stewed tomatoes
>   1 teaspoon dried powdered garlic
>   1 teaspoon dried powdered celery
>   2 tablespoons Worcestershire sauce
>   2 tablespoons dried powdered onion
>   1 can (12 ounces) corned beef, broken apart
>   1¼ cups uncooked brown rice

Mix all ingredients together and simmer 45 minutes to 1 hour. Cool. Prepare three trays. Spread plastic wrap or parchment paper lengthwise over each dehydrator tray, and tape each corner with transparent or masking tape. Spread about 3 cups mixture ¼-to ⅜-inch thick on each tray. Dry 5 or 6 hours. Peel mixture off liner, discard liner, and continue drying directly on trays until crisp—about 4 or 5 hours. To reconstitute, add 2 cups water to each 2½ cup (6 ounce) portion. Simmer 15 to 20 minutes. Yield: 4 to 6 servings.

Yum Yum Spaghetti

1 quart (4 cups) home canned stewed tomatoes or 1 can (1 pound,
  12 ounces) stewed tomatoes
¼ cup raw sunflower seeds
¼ cup raw peanuts
1 large bay leaf
1 2/3 cups dried powdered tomato mixed with 2½ cups water
  or 2 cans (8 ounces) tomato sauce mixed with 1 cup water
2 tablespoons dried snipped onion or ½ cup chopped fresh onion
½ to 1 cup sliced dried mushrooms or 1 can (3 ounces) mushrooms
  with liquid
1 tablespoon honey
1 beef bouillon cube
1 teaspoon dried powdered celery
1 teaspoon dried crushed basil
1 teaspoon dried powdered onion
¾ teaspoon dried powdered garlic
½ teaspoon dried crushed dill
½ teaspoon dried crushed oregano
½ teaspoon cumin
¼ teaspoon dried crushed sage
1 tablespoon dried crushed parsley
1 pound package thin spaghetti cooked according to package
  directions and drained
2 quarts (8 cups) water
½ cup grated Romano cheese

Blend 1 cup tomatoes with sunflower seeds and peanuts; set aside.
To remaining 3 cups tomatoes, add all other ingredients except parsley, spaghetti, 2 quarts water and Romano cheese. Simmer 1 hour.
Remove from heat; add to first mixture, with parsley. Add spaghetti;
let stand 30 minutes to blend flavors. Prepare 4 trays. Spread plastic
wrap or parchment paper lengthwise over dehydrator trays, and tape
each corner with transparent or masking tape. Spread about 3 cups
spaghetti mixture on each tray, ¼- to ¾-inch thick. Dry 5 to 6 hours;
peel spaghetti off liner, discard liner, and continue dry directly on
trays 8 or 9 hours, or until dry and brittle. Each tray of spaghetti
(6 ounces) will serve one person generously or may be stored in individually moisture-proof plastic bags.

To reconstitute, add 2 cups water to each 6-ounce bag, or a total of
8 cups for the complete recipe. Simmer slowly 30 to 45 minutes.
Serve with Romano cheese. Serves 4 generously.

Healthy Meal in a Snack

If you are a late riser, take one of these along; they're also good for lunch.

> 2 eggs
> 1 cup diced bananas or peaches
> ½ cup frozen concentrated orange juice, thawed but not diluted
> ½ cup nonfat dry milk powder
> 1 teaspoon vanilla
> 1/3 cup wheat germ, sesame or sunflower seeds, or chopped almonds

Place eggs, bananas or peaches, concentrated orange juice, milk powder, and vanilla in blender. Blend well. Prepare two trays. Spread plastic wrap or parchment paper lengthwise over each dehydrator tray, and tape to each corner of tray with transparent or masking tape. Pour mixture into a rectangular shape on lined tray. Using a rubber scraper, spread ⅛-to-¼ inch thick, approximately 10-by-13 inches. Sprinkle with wheat germ, sesame or sunflower seeds, or chopped almonds. Dry 10 to 12 hours, or until leather pulls away from liners. Roll up and seal ends. Yield: 2 large rolls.

COOKIES OR BARS

Coconut Granola Bars

> 1 recipe Banana Coconut Leather, not dried
> ½ cup granola or rolled oats

Prepare one tray of undried Banana-Coconut Leather. Sprinkle with granola or oatmeal. Dry 8 to 10 hours, until mixture will pull away from liner. Using kitchen shears, cut into 1½-by-2½-inch bars. Yield: approximately 30 bars.

Coconut-Pineapple-Almond Diamonds

> 1 sheet Pineapple Leather, not dried
> 3 tablespoons chopped unsweetened coconut
> 3 tablespoons finely chopped almonds

Prepare one tray of undried Pineapple Leather. Sprinkle with coconut and almonds. Dry 10 to 12 hours, until mixture will pull away from liner. Using kitchen shears, cut into 1½-by-1½-inch diamond shapes. Yield: approximately 48 diamonds.

Heavenly Fruit Bars

    1 recipe Pineapple-Banana Leather, not dried
    ½ cup granola or rolled oats
    ½ cup snipped dried apricot pieces
    2 small apples, chopped, with or without peels and cores

Prepare two trays of undried Pineapple-Banana Leather. Sprinkle each with ¼ cup granola or rolled oats, ¼ cup dried apricot pieces, and 1 apple chopped. Dry 10 to 12 hours, until mixture will pull away from liner. Using kitchen shears, cut into 1½-by-2½-inch bars. Yield: approximately 60 bars.

Pumpkin-Date Bars

    1 sheet Pumpkin Pie Leather, not dried
    ½ cup finely chopped dates
    ½ cup chopped pecans, almonds, walnuts, sunflower seeds
        or dried pumpkin seeds

Prepare one tray of undried Pumpkin Pie Leather. Sprinkle with dates, and nuts or seeds. Dry 10 to 12 hours, or until mixture will pull away from liner. Using kitchen shears, cut into 1½-by-2½-inch bars. Yield: approximately 30 bars.

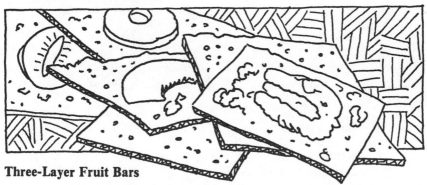

Three-Layer Fruit Bars

    3 tablespoons ground almonds
    1 sheet undried Peach Leather, Apricot Leather, or Strawberry
        Leather
    2/3 cup drained, crushed pineapple
    1 sheet undried Banana Leather
    1½ cups chopped dates
    ¾ cup sunflower seeds
    ½ cup granola or rolled oats

Prepare one tray of undried Peach, Apricot, or Strawberry Leather. Sprinkle with almonds. Dry 8 to 10 hours, until mixture pulls away from liner. Remove from liner.

Prepare one tray of undried Banana Leather. Cover with pineapple. Dry 8 to 10 hours, or until mixture pulls away from liner. Remove liner.

Mix together dates, sunflower seeds, and granola or rolled oats. Spread mixture evenly on the dried Banana Leather and pineapple. Place the dried Peach, Apricot, or Strawberry Leather and almonds directly on top of date mixture. Using kitchen shears, cut through layers, making 1½-by-2-inch bars. Yield: 36 bars.

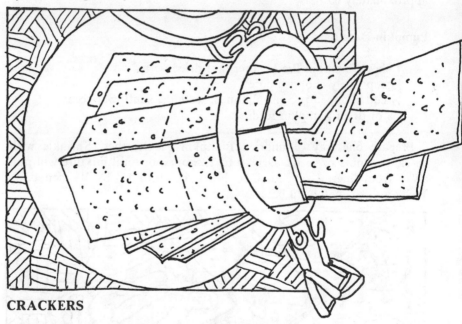

CRACKERS

Honey Graham Crackers

    2 cups freshly ground whole wheat flour, sifted
    2 teaspoons baking powder
    1 teaspoon cinnamon
    ½ cup unsalted butter
    3½ tablespoons honey
    2 to 4 tablespoons milk

Sift together flour, baking powder, and cinnamon. Set aside. Cream together butter, honey, and 2 tablespoons milk. Cut butter mixture into flour mixture, using 2 remaining tablespoons milk if needed.

Using a rolling pin, roll to ¼-inch thickness between sheets of waxed paper. Remove top sheet of waxed paper; cut into 1½-by-1½-inch square or diamond shapes and place on a dehydrator tray. Dry 4 to 6 hours. Yield: about 4 dozen crackers.

Sesame Wheat Crackers

> 1½ cups freshly ground whole wheat flour
> ½ cup seven-grain flour (make seven-grain flour by grinding equal parts of the following together: millet, rye, buckwheat, dried corn, wheat, barley, and brown rice)
> 3 tablespoons honey
> 2 tablespoons apricot or soy oil
> ½ cup dried dates, grated in blender, if desired
> ½ cup water
> 1 tablespoon sesame seeds

Mix wheat flour and seven-grain flour in a bowl. Blend honey, oil, dates, and water; add to flour mixture and mix well. Place mixture between two sheets of waxed paper. Using a rolling pin, roll ¼ inch thick. Remove top sheet of waxed paper; sprinkle mixture with sesame seeds, and press seeds into dough with rolling pin. Cut into 1½-by-1½-inch square or diamond shapes and place on dehydrator tray. Dry 2½ to 3 hours. Yield: about 4 dozen crackers.

FISH

Dried Fish

> 1¼ to 1½ pounds fish
> ¼ cup soy sauce
> 1 tablespoon water
> 1 tablespoon honey
> ½ small clove garlic, crushed
> ⅛ teaspoon grated fresh ginger

Wash fish and blot dry with paper towels. Remove fat, bones, and skin. Slice fish across the grain in strips ¼ inch thick (for easier cutting, freeze fish and thaw enough to slice easily). Mix together remaining ingredients and pour over fish. Distribute marinade well through fish. Refrigerate, covered, 5 hours or overnight. Place fish slices in a single layer on dehydrator tray. Dry about 5 hours or overnight. Store in a cool, dry, dark place in plastic bags or airtight glass jars. Fish will keep a year or so if properly stored. Yield: 6 ounces.

Dried Butterfish or Catfish

    Butterfish or catfish
    1 Q-Tip
    Liquid Smoke

Wash fish and blot dry with paper towels. Remove fat, bones, and skin. Slice fish across grain in strips ⅛ to ¼ inch thick (for easier cutting, freeze fish and thaw enough to slice easily). Dip Q-Tip gently into liquid smoke and put a *very small* amount of liquid smoke on fish. Place fish slices in a single layer on dehydrator tray. Dry 5 or 6 hours. Eat as a snack like Beef Jerky.

Dried Turbot (Fish Jerky)

Do not dehydrate other foods at the same time. Turbot has a marvelous but strong aroma which will permeate other foods.

    1¼ to 1½ pounds turbot
    ¼ cup soy sauce
    2 tablespoons water
    1 tablespoon honey
    ⅛ teaspoon ground ginger

Wash fish and blot dry with paper towels. Remove fat, bones, and skin. Slice fish across the grain ¼ inch thick (for easier cutting, freeze fish and thaw enough to slice easily.) Mix together remaining ingredients and pour over fish. Distribute marinade well through fish. Refrigerate, covered, 5 hours or overnight. Prepare one tray. Spread plastic wrap or parchment paper lengthwise over tray and tape each corner to tray with transparent or masking tape. Place strips in single layer on dehydrator trays. Dry 12 hours, or until fish can readily be pulled off liner. Discard liner and dry fish 12 to 24 hours more until desired crispness. During drying process blot occasionally with paper towels to remove oil from fish. Wrap fish in paper towels and store in glass jars or plastic bags; change paper towels every day or so until most of the oil is absorbed from fish. If storing for longer than a month, it might be wise to freeze fish to avoid stale taste due to their heavy oil content. Yield: about 6 ounces.

Tuna Chip Snacks

    1 cup (6½ ounce can) tuna packed in water, drained
    1 hard cooked egg

1 small Kosher dill pickle
1 tablespoon dill pickle juice
2 tablespoons chopped onion
¼ cup chopped zucchini or celery

Puree all ingredients together in blender using rubber scraper to push down ingredients until blended. Prepare one tray. Spread plastic wrap or parchment paper lengthwise over dehydrator tray and tape each corner to the tray with transparent or masking tape. Spread mixture into a 9-by-13-inch rectangular shape ⅛ to ¼ inch thick. Dry 5 or 6 hours, or until tuna mixture curls and pulls away from liner. Mixture may be pulled away from liner and turned over during drying process. Break or pull off pieces for tuna chips for snacks. Yield: 1 cup chips.

JAMS

Strawberry or Apricot Jam

The freshest tasting jam ever . . . without white sugar! It's delicious on toast, waffles, pancakes, ice cream, cheesecake, and also crepes.

3½ cups whole, cleaned strawberries or apricots, pureed in
blender (about 1¾ cups pureed fruit)
2 tablespoons fresh lemon juice
¼ cup or more honey, depending on sweetness desired

Puree all ingredients in blender. Taste for sweetness, adding more honey if needed. Prepare one tray. Spread plastic wrap or parchment paper lengthwise over tray, and tape each corner to the tray with transparent or masking tape. Spread mixture into a 9-by-13-inch rectangular shape, about ⅜ inch thick. Place in dehydrator. Dry about 3 to 3½ hours until thick like jam. During the drying process, top of puree will become thick so about once an hour, with the flat side of a table knife, mix it into the bottom of puree which is not yet thick. Once mixture is the thickness of jam, pour it into a glass jar and refrigerate. Don't be concerned if some parts of the mixture are a little dryer than others; it will even out in storage.

Ordinarily, we never refrigerate dehydrated foods, but this is not fully dehydrated and will only keep if refrigerated for short term (a few weeks) or frozen for long term (three months to a year). Yield: ½ cup plus 2 tablespoons jam.

Fruit Jam

In recipe for Strawberry or Apricot Jam substitute 3½ cups (1¾ cups pureed) of any of the following fruits instead of strawberries or apricots:

Boysenberries, blackberries, raspberries (if desired, seeds may be removed by straining before puree is poured on dehydrator tray), plums, pineapple, apples, peaches, blueberries, mulberries, honeydew melon, cantaloupe, watermelon, papaya, nectarines, persimmons, pears, oranges or loganberries.

Pineapples, persimmons, honeydews, cantaloupes, watermelons, papayas, blueberries, apples, and pears will probably be sweet enough without adding honey—taste puree to decide. Remember that when part of the water is removed, it will taste sweeter. If any of the fruits taste too sweet, add a little more fresh lemon juice.

LEATHERS

This delightful delicacy with the strange name is the kind Guernseys might not know what to make of. You can see from the number I have included that the possibilities are limitless. Fruit leathers can be eaten instead of candy as snacks or dessert, put into ice cream, pudding, pie, yogurt, or toppings (see next chapter). To make tasty, crispy chips, puree vegetables and dry as another kind of leather treat. There are various ways to pack determined by the length of time you wish to store them. Except for Banana-Peanut Butter Leather, which has its own directions, instructions for storage are in Chapter 5.

Apple or Pear Leather

> 1½ cups diced apple or pear, with or without peel and core (about 1¼ cups pureed)
> 1 tablespoon fresh lemon juice
> ⅛ teaspoon cinnamon
> ⅛ teaspoon freshly ground nutmeg
> 2 tablespoons chopped unsweetened coconut, if desired

Puree apple or pear and lemon juice in blender, pushing apples or pears down with rubber scraper until blended. Prepare one tray. Spread plastic wrap or parchment paper lengthwise over dehydrator tray and tape each corner to tray with transparent or masking tape. Pour mixture into rectangular shape on lined tray. Using rubber scraper, spread ⅛ to ¼ inch thick making one rectangle approximately 9-by-12 inches. Sprinkle with cinnamon and nutmeg, and coconut if desired. Dehydrate 8 to 10 hours, or until leather will pull away from liner. Yield: 1 leather.

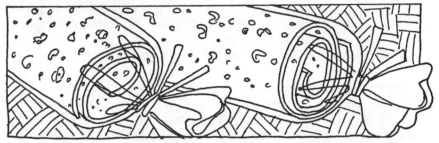

Apple Leather Made with Cherry, Strawberry, or Raspberry Juice

1½ cups diced apples, with or without peel and core (about 1¼ cups pureed)
½ cup dark, sweet cherry juice, or juice from frozen strawberries or raspberries
¼ cup chopped almonds

Puree apples and juice in blender. Prepare one tray. Spread plastic wrap or parchment paper lengthwise over dehydrator tray and tape each corner to tray with transparent or masking tape. Pour mixture into a rectangular shape on lined tray. Using rubber scraper, spread ⅛ to ¼ inch thick, making a rectangle approximately 9-by-13-inches. Sprinkle with almonds. Dehydrate 8 to 10 hours, or until leather will pull away from liner. Yield: 1 leather.

Apricot, Peach, or Nectarine Leather

1½ cups diced apricots, peaches, or nectarines, with or without peel (about 1¼ cups pureed)
1 tablespoon fresh lemon juice
Honey to taste
2 tablespoons chopped or ground almonds, if desired

Puree apricots, peaches, or nectarines and lemon juice in blender. Taste for sweetness. Add honey to taste. Prepare one tray. Spread plastic wrap or parchment paper lengthwise over each dehydrator tray and tape each corner to tray with transparent or masking tape. Pour mixture into one rectangular shape on lined tray. Using rubber scraper, spread ⅛ to ¼ inch thick making a rectangle approximately 9 by 13 inches. Sprinkle with almonds. Dehydrate 8 to 10 hours, or until leather pulls away from liner. Yield: 1 leather.

Apricot-Pineapple Leather

1½ cups apricot halves with or without peel (about 1¼ cups pureed)
1½ cups diced fresh pineapple or drained, unsweetened, canned
    pineapple (about 1¼ cups pureed)
2 tablespoons brandy (if desired) or 1 teaspoon brandy flavoring

Puree all ingredients in blender. Prepare two trays. Spread plastic wrap or parchment paper lengthwise over each dehydrator tray with transparent or masking tape. Pour mixture into two rectangular shapes on lined trays. Using rubber scraper, spread ⅛ to ¼ inch thick making rectangles approximately 9 by 13 inches. Dehydrate 8 to 10 hours, or until leather will pull away from liner. Yield: 2 leathers.

Banana-Peanut Butter Leather

2 large bananas
¼ cup crunchy peanut butter

Puree bananas in blender, add peanut butter. Spread plastic wrap or parchment paper lengthwise over dehydrator tray, and tape each corner to tray with transparent or masking tape. Pour mixture into a rectangular shape about 9 by 13 inches. Spread ⅛ to ¼ inch thick using a rubber scraper. Dehydrate about 8 to 10 hours or until leather will pull away from liner. Discard liner, turn leather over and dry 2 or 3 hours longer. Yield: 1 leather. Special storing instructions: roll up in plastic wrap and seal ends. Leather will keep three to four weeks in a cool, dry, dark place (fat in peanut butter will turn rancid if kept longer) or keep in freezer for six months to a year.

Banana-Coconut Leather

1½ cups diced bananas (2 or 3) to make about 1¼ cups pureed
1 tablespoon fresh lemon juice
2 tablespoons chopped unsweetened coconut if desired

Puree bananas and lemon juice in blender. Prepare one tray. Spread plastic wrap or parchment paper lengthwise over dehydrator tray and tape each corner to tray with transparent or masking tape. Pour mixture into a rectangular shape on the lined tray. Using rubber scraper, spread ⅛ to ¼ inch thick, making a rectangle approximately 9 by 13 inches. Sprinkle with coconut. Dehydrate 8 to 10 hours, or until leather will pull away from liner. Yield: 1 leather.

Blueberry-Banana Leather

1½ cups diced bananas (about 1¼ cups pureed)
1½ cups blueberries (about 1¼ cups pureed)
2 tablespoons fresh lemon juice

Puree all ingredients in blender. Prepare two trays. Spread plastic wrap or parchment paper lengthwise over each dehydrator tray and tape each corner to tray with transparent or masking tape. Pour mixture into two rectangular shapes on lined trays. Using rubber scraper, spread ⅛ to ¼ inch thick making two rectangles approximately 9 by 13 inches. Dehydrate 8 to 10 hours, or until leather will pull away from liner. Yield: 2 leathers.

Sour Cherry Leather

1½ cups pitted red sour cherries (about 1¼ cups pureed)
¼ cup honey or to taste
2 tablespoons ground almonds or unsweetened chopped coconut, if desired.

Puree cherries in blender. Add honey and blend. Prepare one tray. Spread plastic wrap or parchment paper lengthwise over dehydrator tray, and tape each corner to tray with transparent or masking tape. Pour mixture into a rectangular shape on lined tray. Using rubber scraper, spread ⅛ to ¼ inch thick making a rectangle approximately 9 by 13 inches. Sprinkle with almonds or coconut. Dehydrate 8 to 10 hours or until leather will pull away from liner. Yield: 1 leather.

Cherry-Banana Leather

1½ cup fresh or frozen unsweetened dark, sweet cherries, thawed (about 1½ cups pureed)
1½ cups diced bananas (about 1¼ cups pureed)
2 tablespoons fresh lemon juice.

Puree all ingredients in blender. Prepare two trays. Spread plastic wrap or parchment paper lengthwise over each dehydrator tray, and tape each corner to tray with transparent or masking tape. Pour mixture into two rectangular shapes on lined trays. Using rubber scraper, spread ⅛ to ¼ inch thick making two rectangles approximately 9 by 13 inches. Dehydrate 8 to 10 hours or until leather will pull away from liner. Yield: 2 leathers.

Cherry, Blueberry, or Boysenberry Leather

1½ cups pitted cherries, blueberries, or boysenberries
1 tablespoon fresh lemon juice

Puree cherries, blueberries, or boysenberries and lemon juice in blender. Prepare one tray. Spread plastic wrap or parchment paper lengthwise over dehydrator tray, and tape each corner to tray with transparent or masking tape. Pour mixture into a rectangular shape on lined tray. Using rubber scraper, spread ⅛ to ¼ inch thick making a rectangle approximately 9 by 13 inches. Dehydrate 8 to 10 hours, or until leather will pull away from liner. Yield: 1 leather.

Cranberry Applesauce Leather

1 cup fresh cranberries
1 cup unsweetened applesauce
¾ cup frozen concentrated orange juice undiluted

Puree all ingredients in blender. Prepare two trays. Spread plastic wrap or parchment paper lengthwise over each dehydrator tray and tape each corner to tray with transparent or masking tape. Pour mixture into two rectangular shapes on lined trays. Using rubber scraper, spread ⅛ to ¼ inch thick, making two rectangles approximately 9 by 13 inches. Dehydrate 8 to 10 hours or until leather will away from liner. Yield: 2 leathers.

Cranberry Orange Leather

¾ cup fresh cranberries
1 organically grown, unwaxed orange, with peel and white
    part removed
1 very ripe banana
Honey, if necessary, to taste

Puree all ingredients in blender. Taste for sweetness. If the banana is fully ripe, the leather will be sweet enough when dried. If the banana is not fully ripe, you may wish to add a little honey. Prepare one tray. Spread plastic wrap or parchment paper lengthwise over dehydrator tray and tape each corner to tray with transparent or masking tape. Pour mixture into a rectangular shape on lined tray. Using rubber scraper, spread ⅛ to ¼ inch thick making a rectangle approximately 9 by 13 inches. Dehydrate 8 to 10 hours, or until leather will pull away from liner. Yield: 1 leather.

Grape Leather

  1½ cups any variety grapes, washed, with skins and seeds
      (about 1¼ cups pureed)

Puree grapes in blender until seeds and skins are well blended and smooth. Seeds may be a little crunchy in finished leather, but they contain all of the nutrition for the next generation. They should be good for you too. Seeds may be strained out, if desired. Prepare one tray. Spread plastic wrap or parchment paper lengthwise over dehydrator tray, and tape each corner to tray with transparent or masking tape. Pour mixture into a rectangular shape on lined tray. Using rubber scraper, spread ⅛ to ¼ inch thick making a rectangle approximately 9 by 13 inches. Dehydrate 8 to 10 hours or until leather will pull away from liner. Yield: 1 leather.

Grape Banana Leather

  1½ cups grapes, washed, with skins and seeds (about 1¼ cups
      pureed)
  1½ cups diced bananas (about 1¼ cups pureed)
  2 tablespoons fresh lemon juice

Puree grapes in blender until seeds (you may remove them first if you wish) and skins are finely chopped; the seeds will be crunchy like nuts. Add banana and lemon juice and blend well. Prepare two trays. Spread plastic wrap or parchment paper lengthwise over each dehydrator tray, and tape each corner to tray with transparent or masking tape. Pour mixture into two rectangular shapes on lined trays. Using rubber scraper, spread ⅛ to ¼ inch thick making two rectangles approximately 9 by 13 inches. Dehydrate 8 to 10 hours, or until leather will pull away from liner. Yield: 2 leathers.

Orange Banana Leather

  1 organically grown, unwaxed orange
  3 large bananas
  2 tablespoons fresh lemon juice
  Honey to taste
  ⅛ teaspoon cinnamon
  ⅛ teaspoon freshly ground nutmeg, if desired
  ⅛ teaspoon mace, if desired
  4 tablespoons chopped, unsweetened coconut, if desired

Cut thin outer orange peel from ½ of orange and place in blender. Cut off remaining peel and white bitter peel; discard. Puree remaining orange with seeds (they are nutritious) bananas, and lemon juice in blender. Mixture should make about 2½ cups fruit pulp. Taste for sweetness. Add honey if desired. Prepare two trays. Spread plastic wrap or parchment paper lengthwise over each dehydrator tray, and tape each to tray with transparent or masking tape. Pour mixture into two rectangular shapes on lined trays. Using rubber scraper, spread ⅛ to ¼ inch thick making two rectangles approximately 9 by 13 inches. Sprinkle with cinnamon and nutmeg or mace, or coconut if desired. Dehydrate 8 to 10 hours or until leather will pull away from liner. Yield: 2 leathers.

Persimmon-Orange Leather

Substitute 1¾ cups pureed persimmon pulp for three large bananas in the recipe for Orange-Banana Leather.

Pineapple Leather

1½ cups diced fresh pineapple or drained unsweetened canned pineapple (about 1¼ cups pureed)

Puree pineapple in blender. Prepare one tray. Spread plastic wrap or parchment paper lengthwise over dehydrator tray and tape each corner to tray with transparent or masking tape. Pour mixture into a rectangular shape on a lined tray. Using rubber scraper, spread ⅛ to ¼ inch thick making a rectangle approximately 9 by 13 inches. Dehydrate 8 to 10 hours or until leather will pull away from liner. Yield: 1 leather.

Pineapple-Banana Leather

1½ cups diced fresh pineapple or unsweetened canned drained
    pineapple (about 1¼ cups pureed)
1½ cups diced ripe bananas (about 3 bananas or 1¼ cups pureed)

Puree pineapple and bananas in blender. Prepare two trays. Spread plastic wrap or parchment paper lengthwise over each dehydrator tray, and tape each corner to tray with transparent tape. Pour mixture into two rectangular shapes on lined trays. Using rubber scraper, spread ⅛ to ¼ inch thick making two rectangles approximately 9 by 13 inches. Dehydrate 8 to 10 hours, or until leather will pull away from liner. Yield: 2 leathers.

Pink Pineapple Leather

2½ cups diced fresh pineapple or unsweetened canned
    drained pineapple
½ cup strawberries

Puree pineapple and strawberries in blender (about 2½ cups puree). Prepare two trays. Spread plastic wrap or parchment paper lengthwise over each dehydrator tray, and tape each corner to tray with transparent or masking tape. Pour mixture into two rectangular shapes on lined trays. Using rubber scraper, spread ⅛ to ¼ inch thick making two rectangles approximately 9 by 13 inches. Dehydrate 8 to 10 hours or until leather will pull away from liner. Yield: 2 leathers.

Plum Leather

1½ cups pitted plums (about 1¼ cups pureed)
1 tablespoon fresh orange or lemon juice
Honey to taste
1 tablespoon sesame seeds, if desired.

Puree plums and lemon juice in blender. Taste and add honey if necessary. Blend well. Prepare one tray. Spread plastic wrap or parchment paper lengthwise over dehydrator tray, and tape each corner to tray with transparent or masking tape. Pour mixture into a rectangular shape on lined tray. Using rubber scraper, spread ⅛ to ¼ inch thick making a rectangle approximately 9 by 13 inches. Sprinkle with sesame seeds. Dehydrate 8 to 10 hours, or until leather will pull away from liner. Yield: 1 leather.

Pomegranate Leather

> 1½ cups pomegranate seeds
> ¾ cup diced, fresh or unsweetened crushed drained pineapple
> 1 large or 2 medium bananas

Puree pomegranate seeds in blender until seeds are finely chopped; they will be crunchy like nuts. Add pineapple and banana, and blend well. Prepare two trays. Spread plastic wrap or parchment paper lengthwise over each dehydrator tray, and tape each corner to tray with transparent or masking tape. Pour mixture into two rectangular shapes on lined trays. Using rubber scraper, spread ⅛ to ¼ inch thick making two rectangles approximately 9 by 13 inches. Dehydrate 8 to 10 hours or until leather will pull away from liner. Yield: 2 leathers.

Pumpkin Pie Leather

> 2 eggs
> 1 can (1 pound) pumpkin
> 1/3 cup honey
> 1 teaspoon ground cinnamon
> ½ teaspoon ground ginger
> ¼ teaspoon ground cloves
> 1 2/3 cups unsweetened evaporated milk

Place in blender in order given. Blend well. Prepare five trays. Spread plastic wrap or parchment paper lengthwise over each dehydrator tray, and tape each corner to tray with transparent or masking tape. Pour mixture into five rectangular shapes on lined trays. Using rubber scraper, spread approximately ⅛ inch thick making five rectangles approximately 9 by 13 inches. Dehydrate 8 to 10 hours, or until leather will pull away from liner. Yield: 5 leathers.

Raspberry Leather

1½ cups raspberries (about 1¼ cups pureed)

Puree raspberries in blender. Strain to remove seeds, if desired, although seeds contain the nutrition for the next generation so you may wish to leave them in. Prepare one tray. Spread plastic wrap or parchment paper lengthwise over dehydrator tray, and tape each corner to tray with transparent or masking tape. Pour mixture into rectangular shape on lined tray. Using rubber scraper, spread ⅛ to ¼ inch thick making a rectangle approximately 9 by 13 inches. Dehydrate 8 to 10 hours, or until leather will pull away from liner. Yield: 1 leather.

Raspberry-Banana Leather

1½ cups raspberries (about 1¼ cups pureed)
1½ cups bananas (about 1¼ cups pureed)

Puree the strawberries in blender. Add lemon juice and honey to taste. seeds; however, seeds are nutritious if left in leather. Add bananas and blend together. Prepare two trays. Spread plastic wrap or parchment paper lengthwise over dehydrator tray, and tape each corner to tray with transparent or masking tape. Pour mixture into two rectangular shapes on lined trays. Using rubber scraper, spread ⅛ to ¼ inch thick making two rectangles approximately 9 by 13 inches. Dehydrate 8 to 10 hours, or until leather will pull away from liner. Yield: 2 leathers.

Favorite Strawberry or Boysenberry Leather

1½ cups strawberries or boysenberries (about 1¼ cups pureed)
1 tablespoon fresh lemon juice
Honey to taste
2 tablespoons chopped unsweetened coconut, if desired

Puree the berries in blender. Add lemon juice and honey to taste. Prepare one tray. Spread plastic wrap or parchment paper lengthwise over dehydrator tray, and tape each corner to tray with transparent or masking tape. Pour mixture into a rectangular shape on lined tray. Using rubber scraper, spread ⅛ to ¼ inch thick making a rectangle approximately 9 by 13 inches. Sprinkle with chopped coconut. Dehydrate 8 to 10 hours, or until leather will pull away from liner. Yield: 1 leather.

Strawberry-Rhubarb Leather

    1½ cups strawberries (about 1¼ cups pureed)
    1½ cups fresh raw rhubarb (about 1¼ cup pureed)
    Honey to taste

Puree strawberries and rhubarb in blender. Add honey to taste. Prepare two trays. Spread plastic wrap or parchment paper lengthwise over each dehydrator tray, and tape each corner to tray with transparent or masking tape. Pour mixture into two rectangular shapes on lined trays. Using rubber scraper, spread ⅛ to ¼ inch thick making two rectangles approximately 9 by 13 inches. Dehydrate 8 to 10 hours, or until leather will pull away from liner. Yield: 2 leathers.

Strawberry-Pineapple-Banana Leather

    1 cup strawberries
    1 cup fresh pineapple or canned unsweetened pineapple
    1 cup diced bananas
    2 tablespoons fresh lemon juice
    Honey to taste
    ⅛ teaspoon cinnamon, if desired
    ⅛ teaspoon freshly ground nutmeg, if desired
    ⅛ teaspoon mace, if desired
    4 tablespoons chopped unsweetened coconut, if desired

Puree first four ingredients in blender. Taste. Mixture may be sweet enough, depending on ripeness of banana; the mixture will be sweeter when concentrated and dried. Add honey, if desired, to taste. Pureed mixture should be about 2½ cups. Prepare two trays. Spread plastic wrap or parchment paper lengthwise over each dehydrator tray, and tape each corner of wrap or parchment paper to tray, with transparent or masking tape. Pour mixture into two rectangular shapes on lined trays. Using rubber scraper, spread ⅛ to ¼ inch thick making two rectangles approximately 9 by 13 inches. Sprinkle with cinnamon and nutmeg or mace or coconut if desired. Dehydrate 8 to 10 hours or until leather will pull away from liner. Yield: 2 leathers.

Watermelon-Fruit Leather

    1 cup diced watermelon
    1 cup diced banana
    1 cup diced fresh pineapple or canned unsweetened pineapple
    2 tablespoons fresh lemon juice

Puree all ingredients in blender. Prepare two trays. Spread plastic wrap or parchment paper lengthwise over dehydrator tray, and tape each corner to tray with transparent or masking tape. Pour mixture into two rectangular shapes on lined trays. Using rubber scraper, spread ⅛ to ¼ inch thick making two rectangles approximately 9 by 13 inches. Dehydrate 8 to 10 hours or until leather will pull away from liner. Yield: 2 leathers.

Rosy Fruit Leather

    1 cup fresh strawberries, washed
    1 cup fresh apricot halves, unpeeled
    1 cup diced banana
    2 tablespoons fresh lemon juice
    Honey to taste

Puree all ingredients except honey in blender. Taste for sweetness; add honey, if needed, to sweeten. Blend well. Prepare two trays. Spread plastic wrap or parchment paper lengthwise over each dehydrator tray and tape each corner to tray with transparent or masking tape. Pour mixture into two rectangular shapes on lined trays. Using rubber scraper, spread ⅛ to ¼ inch thick making two rectangles approximately 9 by 13 inches. Dehydrate 8 to 10 hours or until leather will pull away from liner. Yield: 2 leathers.

Fruit Salad Leather

>   1 cup grapes, washed, including skins and seeds
>   ½ cup strawberries
>   1 apple, cut in pieces, with or without peel and core
>   ½ pear, cut in pieces, with or without peel and core
>   ½ banana, cut in pieces
>   1 teaspoon honey

Puree all ingredients in blender. Prepare three trays. Spread plastic wrap or parchment paper over each dehydrator tray, and tape each corner to tray with transparent or masking tape. Pour mixture into three rectangular shapes on lined trays. Using rubber scraper, spread ⅛ to ¼ inch thick making three rectangles approximately 9 by 13 inches. Dehydrate 8 to 10 hours, or until leather will pull away from liner. Yield: 3 leathers.

Golden Fruit Leather

>   1½ cups (2 oranges) organically grown, unwaxed oranges
>   with peel and white part cut away
>   1 cup (1 large) diced fresh pear with or without peel and seeds
>   ½ cup (1 medium) diced banana
>   ½ cup grated unsweetened coconut

Puree orange, pear, and banana in blender. This should be about 2½ cups pulp or puree. If using seeds, blend until finely chopped. Prepare two trays. Spread plastic wrap or parchment paper lengthwise over each dehydrator tray, and tape each corner to tray with transparent or masking tape. Pour mixture into two rectangular shapes on lined trays. Using rubber scraper, spread ⅛ to ¼ inch thick making two rectangles approximately 9 by 13 inches. Sprinkle with coconut. Dehydrate 8 to 10 hours, or until leather will pull away from liner. Yield: 2 leathers.

Tomato Leather

>   1½ cups chopped tomatoes (1¼ cups poureed)

Puree tomatoes in blender. Prepare one tray. Spread plastic wrap on parchment paper lengthwise over dehydrator tray and tape each corner to tray with transparent or masking tape. Pour tomato puree into rectangle ⅛ to ¼ inch thick. Dry 6 to 10 hours. If leather is dried to bendable stage, it can be rolled and used as a leather. If dried longer to brittle, breakable stage, it can be powdered in the blender for use as a dried powdered tomato. Yield: one leather, or about 2½ tablespoons powdered tomato.

Hot Tomato Leather

> ½ to 1 teaspoon chopped fresh hot pepper
> 1 tablespoon chopped fresh onion
> 1 tablespoon chopped green pepper

To recipe for Tomato Leather, add hot pepper and onion to tomato. Sprinkle top of mixture with chopped fresh green pepper.

NOODLES

Homemade Noodles

> 1½ cups freshly ground sifted whole wheat flour or a combination
>   of 1 cup freshly ground wheat, ¼ cup millet or soy, and
>   ¼ cup buckwheat flour
> ¼ teaspoon cream of tartar, if desired
> 2 large eggs
> 3 tablespoons water

Mix flour and cream of tarter; divide in half. Beat together eggs and water and add to half the flour mixture. Blend egg-flour mixture well, then add remaining flour mixture. Mix, then knead on lightly floured board until well blended, using more flour if necessary. Divide ball of dough in half. Roll each ball of dough to ⅛ inch thickness using floured rolling pin. Score (cut almost through) into desired noodle width (about ¼ to ½ inch) and place sheets of scored dough on dehydrator tray. (For lasagne, noodles may be scored or cut 1½ inches wide). Dry for about 2 hours; separate noodles along scored lines and dry 2 or 3 hours longer until dry and brittle (they will break when bent). Store in airtight containers at room temperature. Yield: 7 cups dry noodles (15 ounces). Serves four.

Second Method: After noodles have been rolled out to ⅛ inch thickness, instead of scoring, dry about 15 to 30 minutes or until still easily bendable. (If allowed to dry until brittle, noodles cannot be rolled into a pinwheel and cut into noodles.) Roll noodle sheets as for a pinwheel. Sheets must be dry enough so they will not stick together. Using sharp knife, slice into desired thickness. By this method it is easy to slice noodles very fine (⅛ inch wide), ¼ inch thick for regular noodles, or even 1½ inches wide for lasagne. Once noodles are sliced, separate and place back on dehydrator trays. Dry 3½ to 5 hours longer until dry and brittle.

Spinach or Vegetable Noodles

Substitute ¼ cup dried powdered spinach or a mixture of ¼ cup dried powdered vegetables for ¼ cup of flour or flour mixture in recipe for Homemade Noodles. Vegetables which powder well and are also good for this recipe are broccoli, green beans, tomatoes, and corn. Powdered dried parsley, watercress, onion, and garlic may be used sparingly.

**Spaghetti Sauce
from Tomato Leather**

To recipe for Tomato Leather, add your favorite spices for spaghetti sauce. Dry to brittle, breakable stage. Powder in blender for spaghetti sauce mix. Yield: per leather about 2½ tablespoons.

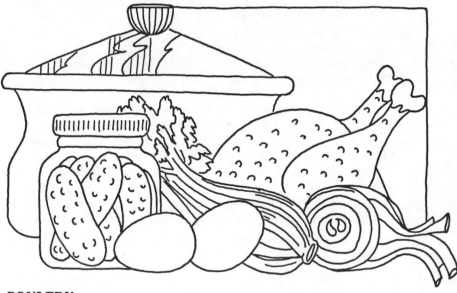

POULTRY

**Chicken Snacks
(for Sandwiches or Snacks)**

    1 (3 1/3 to 4 pound) stewing chicken
    1½ cups celery
    4 hard-cooked eggs, peeled
    4 or 5 small Kosher dill pickles
    1 large onion

Wash and clean chicken. Place in large stewing kettle with water to cover (about 2½ quarts). Cook 1 to 1½ hours, or until tender. Remove skin, bone, and all fat from chicken. (Save broth for making soup.) Grind chicken and all remaining ingredients together, alternating them as they go through the grinder. Mix well. Prepare four trays. Spread plastic wrap or parchment paper lengthwise over dehydrator tray, and tape each corner to tray with transparent or masking tape. Divide chicken mixture in four parts and spread one part on each lined tray about ⅛ to ¼ inch thick. Place trays in dehydrator to dry. Dry 6 to 8 hours. After mixture has dried sufficiently to hold together, it may be removed from liner and placed directly on trays for faster drying. Chicken will retain a beautiful light color. Break or pull off pieces for chips for snacks. Yield: 3½ to 4 sheets of chips or 3½ to 4 cups chips.

Turkey Snacks (for Sandwiches or Snacks)

Substitute 3½ to 4 pounds uncooked turkey for chicken in recipe for Chicken Snacks; 7 cups diced cooked leftover roast turkey may also be used. If amount of leftover turkey is less than 7 cups, cut recipe in half by using:
   3½ cups cooked diced turkey
   ¾ cups celery
   2 hard-cooked eggs, peeled
   2 or 3 small Kosher dill pickles
   1 small onion
Yield: 2 sheets of snacks.

Jerky Made from Turkey (Turkey Jerky)

Children and grownups love this!

   1½ pounds uncooked turkey (preferably breast) with fat,
      skin, and bone removed
   ¼ cup soy sauce
   1 tablespoon fresh lemon juice
   ¼ teaspoon dried powdered garlic
   ¼ teaspoon freshly ground pepper
   ⅛ teaspoon ginger

Slice turkey across grain in strips ⅛ to ¼ inch thick (for easier cutting, freeze meat and thaw enough to slice easily). Mix together remaining ingredients and pour over turkey. Distribute marinade well through turkey. Place turkey on trays in a single layer on dehydrator trays. Dry about 5 hours or overnight. Yield: about 6 ounces.

SNACKS

Fresh Corn Chips

Corn is one of our most nutritious foods. We destroy much of this by turning it to starch when we cook it. Here's a delicious corn chip that is never cooked.

> 2 cups (3 or 4 ears) cut fresh corn (about 1 1/3 cups pureed)
> ¼ teaspoon dried powdered onion, if desired
> ¼ teaspoon dried powdered garlic, if desired
> 3 tablespoons chopped green pepper
> 3 tablespoons chopped tomato, including peel and seeds

Puree corn, onion, and garlic in blender. Prepare one tray. Spread plastic wrap lengthwise over tray, and tape each corner to tray with transparent or masking tape. Pour corn mixture into a rectangular shape on lined tray. Using rubber scraper, spread ¼-inch thick making rectangle about 9 by 13 inches. Sprinkle with green pepper and tomato. Dehydrate 8 to 10 hours or overnight, until crispy and crinkled. Corn mixture may be broken into chips and served in a bowl as a snack or with Homemade Cream Cheese or Tuna Dip. Yield: 1 or more cups of chips.

Corn Tomato Chips

1 cup (1 large or 2 small ears) cut fresh corn (about ¾ cup pureed)
1 cup chopped fresh tomato (about ½ cup pureed)

Puree corn and tomatoes in blender (mixture should make about 1 1/3 cups). Prepare one tray. Spread plastic wrap lengthwise over dehydrator tray, and tape each corner to tray with transparent masking tape. Pour mixture into a rectangular shape on lined tray. Using rubber scraper, spread ¼ inch thick making rectangle about 9 by 13 inches. Dehydrate 8 to 10 hours or overnight, until crispy and crinkled. Corn Tomato mixture may be broken into chips and served in a bowl as a snack as is, or with Homemade Cream Cheese. Yield: 1 or more cups of chips.

Nuts

Raw peanuts, almonds, walnuts, and other varieties are delicious prepared in the dehydrator and can be dried in the shell or unshelled, without the preservatives added to commercial nuts. They keep best if dried in unbroken or uncracked shells. If they are unshelled, place on trays, dry overnight 10 to 14 hours. If shelled, dry 8 to 12 hours, or overnight. May be eaten as snacks, used in Granola, or other recipes.

Homemade Raisins

The most delicious raisins you'll ever eat are the ones you make yourself. Once you prepare your own, you'll never want to purchase commercial ones again, either to snack on or to use in any recipe with raisins. Any variety or color grape may be used.
Wash grapes well; cut in half; remove seeds, if desired. Arrange in a single layer on dehydrator trays. Dry 12 to 24 hours, or until leathery and dry. Raisins will be slightly sticky, but will not stick together if completely dried.

SOUP

Easy Beef Vegetable Soup

Here is what to do with a little bit of leftover stew.

1¼ to 1½ cups leftover beef stew
1 to 1½ cups water or broth
2 tablespoons dried powdered tomato, if desired

Cut away or remove any fat from meat and broth. Puree leftover beef stew in blender until smooth. Prepare one tray. Spread plastic wrap lengthwise over dehydrator tray, and tape each corner to tray with transparent or masking tape. Pour mixture into rectangular shape on lined tray. Using rubber scraper, spread ¼ inch thick, making a rectangle about 9 by 13 inches. Dehydrate 8 to 10 hours or overnight; drying time will vary due to amount of fat in stew. Break or tear into pieces. To serve, puree in blender with water or broth and tomato powder. Heat to serve. Yield: 1 or 2 servings.

YOGURT

Homemade Yogurt (Regular)

Try it! Once you make yogurt yourself you will never again want to buy it. Delicious. All homemade yogurt recipes depend upon a "starter," a small amount of commercial yogurt used as one of the ingredients. Use only plain, unflavored yogurt for starter, and ask your health food store to recommend a brand that has had the least amount of processing. You will be more successful in yogurt-making if, instead of using your own homemade yogurt as the "starter," you use the plain commercial type each time you make a new recipe of yogurt.

> 1 cup raw milk
> 1 tablespoon plain commercial yogurt

Place candy thermometer in milk in a stainless steel or enamel pot. Heat, stirring 2 or 3 times, until thermometer reaches 185 degrees. Cool milk to 130 degrees. Skim off any accumulated film with wooden spoon. Pour milk into glass or crockery (not metal) bowl. Drop yogurt to the bottom of the bowl using a spiral upward motion; stir yogurt to the top of the milk about three times. Remove bottom three shelves of dehydrator and place mixture in bowl on bottom of dehydrator. Do not stir or move yogurt at this stage. Turn on dehydrator. After about 6 to 8 hours, yogurt will become thick. Skim off any film and refrigerate a few hours. Yogurt will thicken more. At this stage, yogurt is ready to eat. Pureed fruit or vegetables may now be added. Yield: 1 cup.

To make 2 cups yogurt, use the following proportions in the above recipe:
> 2 cups raw milk
> 2 tablespoons plain commercial yogurt

To make 4 cups (1 quart) yogurt, use the following proportions in the above recipe:
   4 cups (1 quart) raw milk
   ¼ cup (4 tablespoons) plain commercial yogurt

To make 8 cups (2 quarts) yogurt, use the following proportions in the above recipe:
   8 cups (2 quarts) raw milk
   ½ cup plain commercial yogurt
Two shallow bowls may be necessary to hold 2 quarts of yogurt.

Homemade Yogurt (Creamy)

   1 cup raw milk
   2 tablespoons nonfat dry milk powder
   1½ teaspoons plain commercial yogurt

Place candy thermometer in milk in a stainless steel or enamel pot. Heat, stirring 2 or 3 times, until thermometer reaches 185 degrees. Cool milk to 130 degrees. Skim off any accumulated film with wooden spoon. Add the milk powder, stirring thoroughly. Pour milk into a glass or crockery (not metal) bowl. Drop yogurt to the bottom of the bowl, using a spiral upward motion; stir yogurt to the top of the milk about three times. Remove bottom three shelves of dehydrator and place mixture in bowl on bottom of dehydrator. Turn on dehydrator. Do not stir or move yogurt at this stage. After about 6 to 8 hours, yogurt will become thick. Skim off any film and refrigerate a few hours. Yogurt will thicken more. At this stage, yogurt is ready to eat. Pureed fruit or vegetables may now be added. Yield: 1 cup.

To make 2 cups yogurt, use the following proportions in the above recipe:
   2 cups raw milk
   ¼ cup nonfat dry milk powder
   1 tablespoon plain commercial yogurt

To make 4 cups (1 quart) yogurt, use the following proportions in the above recipe:
   4 cups (1 quart) raw milk
   ½ cup nonfat dry milk powder
   2 tablespoons plain commercial yogurt

To make 8 cups (2 quarts) yogurt, use the following proportions in the above recipe:

8 cups (2 quarts) raw milk
1 cup nonfat dry milk powder
¼ cup (4 tablespoons) plain commercial yogurt
Two shallow bowls may be necessary to hold 2 quarts of yogurt

PET FOOD

Meaty Pet Snacks

When I was making this, my dog refused to eat it when I offered him some midway through the drying process. He had no trouble with it after it was dry and ate it with great relish. Even my cat loved it, preferring the Meaty Pet Snacks, whereas my dog quickly ate both varieties. Pet food is unbelievably easy to make. When your favorite animal wants a treat, rest assured you are feeding him well with these snacks.

1½ cups freshly ground whole wheat flour
2 teaspoons beef bouillon dissolved in ½ cup boiling water
4 sticks Beef Jerky grated in blender or ¼ pound ground beef cooked and drained

Mix all ingredients together. Knead well on a lightly floured board. Roll ⅛ to ¼ inch thick, using floured rolling pin. Place on tray and score into ¾-inch squares, cutting halfway through dough. Dry 2 hours. Remove and either break or cut apart with kitchen shears on scoring lines. Return to dehydrator and continue drying for approximately 5 hours or until dry. Yield: 2½ cups squares.

Sweet Pet Snacks

1 cup freshly ground whole wheat flour
½ cup freshly ground buckwheat flour
½ cup dried dates, grated in blender
1 tablespoon honey
½ cup buttermilk

Mix all ingredients together. Knead well on a lightly floured board. Roll ⅛ to ¼ inch thick, using floured rolling pin. Place on tray and score into ¾-inch squares, cutting halfway through dough. Dry 2 hours. Remove and either break or cut apart with kitchen shears on scoring lines. Return to dehydrator and continue drying for approximately 5 hours or until dry. Yield: 2½ cups squares.

Recipes Using Home-Dried Foods

To increase your eating enjoyment, use your dried products in a variety of breakfast, lunch, and dinner recipes. Recipes referred to elsewhere in the book may be found in the index. Categories included in this chapter are:

Beef

Beverages

Breads, Pancakes, and Waffles

Cakes

Cereals

Desserts

Eggs

Fish

Frostings and Toppings

Ham

Ice Cream

Lamb

Main Dishes

Pie Crusts

Pies

Pork

Poultry

Salads

Sauces

Snacks

Soups

Vegetables

Yogurt

Miscellaneous

BEEF

Golden Gate Pot Roast

> 1 (3 pound) round-bone or seven-bone blade chuck
>   roast
> ½ cup teriyaki sauce
> 1/3 cup sliced dried green pepper
> 1/3 cup dried mushrooms
> 1 teaspoon finely chopped, dried onion
> 1½ cups sliced dried carrots
> 1 tablespoon arrowroot

Place roast on a large sheet (about 2½ feet) of heavy-duty foil in roasting or broiling pan. Shape foil around roast. Add remaining ingredients except arrowroot. Bring the foil ends up around and above roast; fold over as for package wrap. Fold ends and bring to the top of wrapped meat. Meat should be completely wrapped and covered by foil. Bake at 350 degrees 2 to 2½ hours for medium roast, 3 hours for well-done roast. Open foil; pour liquid into a 2-cup measure. Add enough water to make 2 cups. Add arrowroot to liquid. Cook, stirring constantly, until thickened and clear. Serve gravy with roast and vegetables. 8 to 12 servings.

Pepper Steak

> 1½ pound top round steak, tenderized (or cut 1-by-½-by-2½
>   inch strips from a seven-bone roast)
> 2 tablespoons apricot or soy oil
> 4 tablespoons soy sauce
> 3 tablespoons dried powdered tomato mixed with 3
>   tablespoons water
> 1 cup dried broken tomato slices soaked in 1 cup
>   water 10 minutes
> 2/3 cup dried broken pieces green pepper
>   soaked in 2/3 cup water 30 minutes
> ½ teaspoon freshly ground or coarse ground pepper
> ½ teaspoon dried powdered garlic or 1 clove garlic, minced
> ¼ teaspoon honey
> ⅛ teaspoon powdered ginger
> 1 teaspoon dried powdered or flaked onion
> ½ cup beef consomme mixed with ½ cup water
> 2 tablespoons cornstarch

Tenderize round steak by pounding (if using meat from a seven-bone roast, no need to pound). Cut meat diagonally into strips. Heat oil in frying pan. When hot, add meat and brown quickly. Add remaining ingredients, except consomme mixed with water, and cornstarch. Cover and simmer 20 minutes. Blend cornstarch, consomme and water. Add a little of hot liquid from meat to cornstarch mixture; then add all to meat. Cook, stirring constantly, until thickened and clear. Serve over hot rice. 6 servings.

Easy Chili

1½ pounds ground beef
2 cups water
1 tablespoon chili powder
1 tablespoon curry powder
½ cup dried powdered tomato
1 can (1 pound 13 ounces or 3½ cups) kidney beans and
    liquid or 3½ cups pinto bean sprouts
1½ cups grated sharp cheddar cheese or 1 cup dried cheddar
    cheese powder blended with 6 tablespoons water
6 to 12 tablespoons chopped fresh onion

In a frying pan, saute ground beef in its own fat until lightly browned. Pour off drippings. Add water, chili, and curry powders. Simmer 5 to 10 minutes. Blend in tomato powder. Add kidney beans or pinto bean sprouts. To keep fresh tomato flavor, heat only until hot enough to serve. Pour into serving bowls. Top each serving with ¼ cup grated cheese or 2 tablespoons dried cheese and water mixture. Sprinkle each with 1 or 2 tablespoons onions. Yield: 6½ cups. 6 servings.

Pear-Topped Meat Loaf

½ cup milk
½ cup stuffing crumbs
3 tablespoons dried powdered tomato mixed with 3
    tablespoons water
1½ pounds ground beef
1/3 cup chopped dried onion
1 teaspoon soy sauce
1/3 cup water chestnuts, drained and sliced
10 to 20 round, cored, cross-cut dried pear slices
½ cup (4 ounces) Homemade Yogurt
Tiny sprigs of fresh watercress or parsley

Mix milk, stuffing crumbs, and tomato mixture together. In another bowl combine beef, onion, soy sauce, and water chestnuts. Combine the two mixtures. Place pears on bottom of a buttered 3-by-5-by-8-inch baking dish. Pack meat mixture carefully around pears. Bake at 350 degrees for 1 hour. Invert on serving platter. Fill centers of pear slices with a blob of yogurt. Place a tiny sprig of watercress or parsley in the center of each blob of yogurt. 6 to 8 servings.

BEVERAGES

Apple Smoothie

¾ cup dried apple
1 cup apple juice
1 cup (8 ounces) Homemade Yogurt
2 tablespoons honey, if desired
⅛ teaspoon cinnamon, if desired
½ cup crushed ice

Puree dried apple and apple juice in blender. Add yogurt, honey to taste, cinnamon, and crushed ice. 2 or 3 servings.

Banana Shake

½ cup dried banana chips
1½ cups raw milk
½ teaspoon vanilla, if desired
1 cup crushed ice, if desired

Puree dried bananas in ½ cup milk. Add remaining 1 cup milk, vanilla, and ice. 2 servings.

Banana Carob Shake

Add 3 tablespoons raw carob powder to Banana Shake recipe.

Banana Smoothie

½ cup dried banana chips
1 cup raw milk
1 cup (8 ounces) Homemade Yogurt
2 tablespoons honey, if desired
½ teaspoon vanilla, if desired
1 cup crushed ice

Puree dried bananas in ½ cup milk. Add remaining ingredients. 2 or 3 servings.

Banana Carob Smoothie

Add 3 tablespoons raw carob powder to Banana Smoothie recipe.

Hot Mulled Cranberry Juice

1 cup dried cranberry halves
4 cups apple juice
½ teaspoon dried powdered orange rind
¼ teaspoon dried powdered lemon rind
¼ teaspoon cinnamon
⅛ teaspoon freshly grated nutmeg
Honey to taste, if desired
4 cinnamon sticks

Puree dried cranberries in blender with 1 cup of apple juice. In a saucepan mix remaining 3 cups apple juice with all other ingredients except cinnamon sticks. Heat to 190 degrees or almost to a boil. Remove from heat and pour into 4 serving cups or mugs using cinnamon sticks as stirrers. 4 servings.

Hawaiian Delight

> 4 cups pineapple juice
> 2½ cups apple juice
> 1/3 cup dried cranberry halves pureed in blender with
>   1/3 cup water until smooth
> Honey to taste, if desired
> 1 cup finely chopped coconut
> Pineapple cubes
> Mint sprigs

Mix all ingredients except pineapple and mint. Pour into mugs over crushed ice. Add a bamboo stirrer to each; top with a pineapple cube and a sprig of mint. 4 to 5 servings.

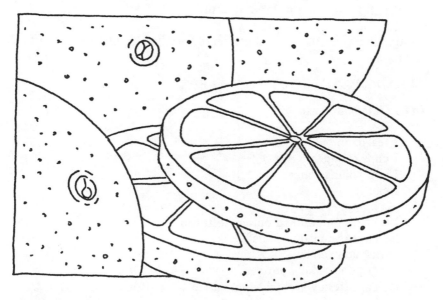

Orange Juice

> 1 cup dried powdered orange without peel
> 2 cups water

Mix, shake, or blend orange and water together. Chill to serve. 2 servings of 1 cup each.

Pineapple Fruit Smoothie

½ cup dried banana, strawberry, apricot, peach, pear, or apple slices
1 cup unsweetened pineapple juice
1 cup (8 ounces) Homemade Yogurt
2 or more tablespoons honey, if desired
½ cup crushed ice

Puree dried fruit and pineapple juice in blender. Add yogurt and honey to taste (honey may not be needed for banana, pear, or apple blends). Blend in crushed ice. 2 or 3 servings.

Tomato Juice

1 cup dried powdered tomato
6 to 8 cups water
⅛ teaspoon pepper, if desired
Fresh lemon juice to taste, if desired

Mix, shake, or blend all ingredients together. Chill to serve. 6 to 8 servings.

BREADS, PANCAKES, AND WAFFLES

Indio Date Nut Bread

1 teaspoon baking soda
2 cups chopped pitted dates
1 cup boiling water
1 egg
½ cup honey
1 tablespoon unsalted butter, softened
1½ cups chopped walnuts
1 teaspoon vanilla
½ teaspoon baking powder
1½ cups freshly ground sifted whole wheat flour

Sprinkle soda over dates; add boiling water. Let stand until cool. Beat egg with honey, butter, nuts, and vanilla. Then mix this with date-water mixture. In a separate bowl, mix baking powder and flour; sift. Add this dry mixture to the other ingredients; mix thoroughly. Place batter in 5-by-8-inch greased loaf pan. Bake at 350 degrees 50 to 55 minutes. Allow to cool before slicing. If desired, slice thin and serve with Homemade Cream Cheese.

Pumpkin Bread

Here's a bread that uses the abundance of fall apples and pumpkin.

    1 1/3 cups apricot oil, soy oil, or unsalted
       melted butter
    1 cup honey
    4 eggs, beaten
    1½ cups dried apples, with or without peel and core
    1 1/3 cups unsweetened pineapple juice
    1¼ cups uncooked dried pumpkin or banana squash
       pieces, pureed until smooth in blender with
       1¼ cups water (if dried pumpkin or squash is
       not available, 1½ cups canned pumpkin may be used)
    3 1/3 cups freshly ground sifted whole wheat flour
    1 tablespoon baking powder
    2 teaspoons baking soda
    1½ teaspoons cinnamon
    ¾ teaspoon freshly ground nutmeg
    ½ teaspoon mace
    1½ cups chopped walnuts or pecans

Beat together oil or melted butter, honey and eggs. Place dried apples in blender; pour pineapple juice over apples and blend or puree until smooth. Add to egg mixture. Also add pureed pumpkin or squash and mix well. Sift together flour, baking powder, soda, cinnamon, nutmeg, and mace and add to first mixture, blending well. Stir in walnuts. Pour into a greased, floured 10-inch tube pan. Bake at 350 degrees for 1 hour.

Zucchini Bread

Drying lots of grated zucchini is worthwhile just to make this recipe!

    3 eggs, beaten
    1 cup apricot oil, soy oil, or unsalted butter
    1 cup honey
    2 teaspoons vanilla
    3 cups freshly ground sifted whole wheat flour
    2 teaspoons baking soda
    ½ teaspoon baking powder
    1½ teaspoons cinnamon
    ¾ teaspoon freshly ground nutmeg

2 cups shredded dried zucchini
1 can (8½ ounces) unsweetened crushed pineapple
1 cup chopped black or English walnuts
1 cup currants

Blend eggs, oil or melted butter, honey, and vanilla. Sift together flour, soda, baking powder, cinnamon, and nutmeg. Add dry ingredients to egg mixture, beating well until thick and foamy. Mix zucchini with pineapple and add to first mixture. Stir in walnuts and currants. Place in two greased and floured 4½-by-8½-inch loaf pans. Bake at 350 degrees for 1 hour. Cool 10 minutes. Turn out on racks. Slice thinly with serrated knife to serve. Yield: 2 loaves.

Bran Muffins

¼ cup apricot or soy oil
1 egg
1 cup milk or soy milk
2 tablespoons blackstrap molasses
2 tablespoons lecithin, if desired
1 cup bran

1 tablespoon baking powder
1½ cups freshly ground sifted whole wheat flour

½ cup dried apricot or pineapple pieces,
    soaked in 1/3 cup·water 1 or 2 hours or overnight
    (½ cup raisins or chopped dates, not soaked, may be used
    instead of apricots)
Carob powder, cinnamon, or nutmeg

Mix together oil, egg, milk, molasses, lecithin, and bran. Sift together baking powder and flour and add to first mixture. Mix in apricot or pineapple. Fill oiled, floured muffin tins two-thirds full. Bake at 400 degrees for 25 minutes. Sprinkle with carob powder, cinnamon, or nutmeg. Yield: 10 to 12 muffins.

Apple Buttermilk Pancakes

1 cup rolled oats
1 cup freshly ground sifted whole wheat flour
¼ cup sesame seeds or wheat germ
¼ cup nonfat dry milk powder
1 teaspoon baking soda
2 eggs
2 cups buttermilk
1 tablespoon honey
¼ cup apricot oil, soy oil or melted unsalted
    butter
1 cup dried apples, with or without peel and core,
    pureed in blender with ½ cup warm water

Mix together the first five dry ingredients. Beat together with a fork eggs, buttermilk, and honey; add to first mixture, mixing well. Stir in oil or melted butter and apples. Drop batter from spoon onto a lightly greased griddle or heavy frying pan (the griddle or frying pan is hot enough when a few drops of cold water dance on the surface) and bake until top is bubbly around edges and lightly browned on the bottom. Turn only once. Yield: 10 to 12 pancakes. Serve with Hot Honey Butter (heat ½ cup unsalted butter with ½ cup honey).

Banana Buttermilk Pancakes

Omit 1 cup dried apples pureed in ½ cup warm water in Apple Buttermilk Pancakes. Add 1 cup dried banana chips to batter or sprinkle dried banana chips on unbrowned side of pancakes just before turning.

Brussels Apricot-Pecan Waffles

> 2 cups freshly ground sifted whole wheat flour
> 4 eggs, separated
> 5 tablespoons melted unsalted butter
> ½ cup unsweetened pineapple juice
> 2/3 cup milk
> ½ teaspoon vanilla
> ¾ cup thinly sliced dried apricots
>   soaked 1 hour in ¾ cup unsweetened pineapple juice
> 1 cup chopped pecans

Combine flour, egg yolks, butter, pineapple juice, milk, and vanilla in a bowl. Beat until smooth. Add apricots with any liquid and pecans. Whip egg whites until stiff and fold into batter. Spread a little of the batter on a waffle iron and cook. Serve with Hot Honey Butter and Honey Whipped Cream. 4 to 6 servings.

Hot Honey Butter

> ½ cup unsalted butter
> ½ cup honey

Heat until bubbly. Serve hot over waffles or pancakes.

Honey Whipped Cream

> 1 cup whipping cream, whipped
> 2 tablespoons honey
> 1 teaspoon vanilla

Mix all together. Top each waffle with a spoonful or two of mixture on top of Hot Honey Butter.

CAKES

Applesauce Cake with Whipped Cream and Honey Topping

> ¼ cup unsalted butter
> ½ cup honey
> 2 eggs
> 2 tablespoons warm water
> 1 cup dried apples, with or without peel and core,
>   pureed in blender with ½ cup warm water

2½ cups freshly ground sifted whole wheat flour
½ cup cornstarch
1 teaspoon baking soda
1 teaspoon cinnamon
1 teaspoon freshly ground nutmeg
½ teaspoon cloves
1 cup raisins
1 cup chopped walnuts

Blend butter and honey well. Add eggs, water, and apples. Sift together flour, cornstarch, soda, cinnamon, nutmeg, and cloves into first mixture. Blend well. Add raisins and walnuts. Pour into three 4½-by-8½-by-2½-inch loaf pans which have been buttered and lined with brown-paper. Bake at 325 degrees for 45 minutes. Cut into slices and serve each with a spoonful of Whipped Cream and Honey Topping.

Whipped Cream and Honey Topping

1 cup whipping cream, whipped
2 tablespoons mild honey
1 teaspoon vanilla

Mix all ingredients together.

Bourbon Pecan Cake

1 pound shelled pecans, broken into pieces
½ cup raisins, cut in half
½ cup chopped dates
½ cup dried chopped pineapple
1½ cups freshly ground sifted whole wheat flour
1 teaspoon baking powder
½ cup unsalted butter
½ cup plus 1 tablespoon honey
3 eggs, separated
2 teaspoons freshly grated nutmeg
½ cup bourbon or apple juice
Pecan halves for decorating top of cake

Mix together pecans, raisins, dates, and pineapple. Measure 1½ cups sifted flour and sift it twice more. Mix ½ cup of this flour with nuts and raisins; set aside. To remaining cup of flour, add baking powder and sift again. Cream butter with honey; add egg yolks, one at a time, beating well after each addition until smooth and lemon-colored. Soak nutmeg in bourbon or apple juice 10 minutes. Add to creamed mixture alternately with remaining sifted flour, beating thoroughly after each addition until well blended. Fold nut-fruit mixture into batter. Beat egg whites until stiff and fold gently into batter. Butter and flour 3-pound tube pan. Fill with batter; let stand 10 minutes to settle. Decorate top with pecan halves. Bake at 325 degrees for 1½ hours. If top browns too quickly, cover with foil. Let cake stand in pan ½ hour before removing to cake rack to cool. Good eaten immediately if desired, or wrap in bourbon-dampened cloth and store in airtight container.

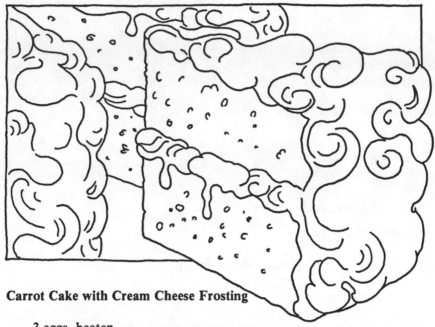

Carrot Cake with Cream Cheese Frosting

> 3 eggs, beaten
> 1½ cups apricot or soy oil
> 1 cup honey
> 2 teaspoons vanilla
> 1 tablespoon yeast dissolved in ½ cup warm water
> 2½ cups freshly ground sifted whole wheat flour
> ½ cup bran
> 1½ teaspoons cinnamon
> ½ teaspoon freshly ground nutmeg
> 1½ cups raisins
> 1 cup grated dried carrots soaked in 1 cup hot
>   water for 5 minutes
> 1 can (12 ounces) crushed pineapple, drained
>   (about 1 cup)
> 1 cup chopped pecans

Mix together eggs, oil, honey, and vanilla. Stir in dissolved yeast. Sift together flour, bran, cinnamon, and nutmeg. Add to first mixture, mixing well. Mix in remaining ingredients. Pour into a greased, floured 9-by-13-inch baking pan. Bake at 350 degrees for 1 hour. Cool. Spread with Cream Cheese Frosting.

Cream Cheese Frosting

1 cup (8 ounces) Cream Cheese
2 tablespoons unsalted butter
¼ cup honey

Cream and beat all ingredients together. Spread evenly on Carrot Cake.

Cranberry-Date Pinwheels

1 dried sheet of any of the Cranberry Leathers
1 cup Homemade Cream Cheese
2 or 3 tablespoon half and half or milk
¾ cup finely chopped dried dates

Add enough half and half or milk to cream cheese to soften. Spread evenly on Cranberry Leather; sprinkle with dates. Beginning with 9-inch side, roll cranberry sheet into a pinwheel. With a very sharp knife or electric knife, cut into ½ to ¾-inch slices. Arrange on plate or platter to serve. Yield: 12 to 18 pinwheels.

Figs in Port

2 cups dried figs
1½ cups water
1 (3-inch) stick cinnamon
1 teaspoon dried powdered orange rind or 2 teaspoons
    freshly grated orange rind
1 tablespoon honey
1 tablespoon fresh lemon juice
½ cup port wine or apple juice

Bring figs, water, cinnamon, and orange rind to a boil. Simmer 10 minutes. Remove from heat. Add honey, lemon juice and wine or apple juice. Cover and refrigerate for 24 hours or longer. Serve chilled with Homemade Yogurt or Homemade Natural Vanilla Ice Cream. 5 or 6 servings.

Orange Delight Cake

2 cups freshly ground sifted whole wheat flour
½ cup cornstarch
1 teaspoon baking soda
¾ cup unsalted butter
¾ cup mild honey
3 eggs
1 cup buttermilk
1 cup raisins
3 tablespoons dry powdered orange peel
½ cup chopped pecans
½ cup chopped walnuts
1 teaspoon vanilla
¾ cup orange juice
¼ cup mild honey
½ teaspoon rum flavoring

Sift flour and cornstarch together three times. Add soda and sift again. Beat butter and ¾ cup honey until fluffy. Add eggs one at a time, beating well after each addition. Add flour alternately with buttermilk one-fourth at a time. Stir in raisins, orange peel, nuts, and vanilla. Pour batter into 9- or 10-inch tube or bundt pan. Bake at 350 degrees 55 minutes. Cool 10 minutes. Remove from pan. While cake is still warm, combine orange juice, ¼ cup honey, and rum flavoring and slowly pour over cake. The cake is best made several days in advance before serving.

CEREALS

Four-Grain Cereal

    2 tablespoons whole wheat
    2 tablespoons soy beans
    2 tablespoons oats
    2 tablespoons golden millet
    1½ to 2 cups water
    ¼ cup sunflower seeds
    16 to 20 almonds, ground
    Dried fruit: apples, dates, raisins, peaches, pears, bananas, etc.

Grind wheat, soy beans, oats, and millet. Mix with 1½ cups water. Cook, stirring occasionally, until grain is tender and thickened. Add ½ cup more water, if needed. Sprinkle each serving with 2 tablespoons sunflower seeds, half of almonds, and dried fruit. Serve with milk. 2 servings.

Seven-Grain Cereal (2 Servings)

    2½ tablespoons whole wheat
    2 tablespoons rye
    1 tablespoon millet
    1 tablespoon brown rice

    1½ teaspoons flax seed
    1½ tablespoons wheat germ
    1 tablespoon cornmeal (made by grinding dried corn in grinder
        or blender)
    1½ to 2 cups water
    Honey to taste and/or dried fruit such as banana chips,
        strawberries, apples, peaches, pears, blueberries, dates,
        prunes, raisins, etc.

Grind whole wheat, rye, millet, brown rice, and flax seed together. Add wheat germ, cornmeal, and water. Bring to a boil in a saucepan. Turn heat down to a simmer and cook, stirring occasionally, until thickened and cereal is tender, about 8 to 10 minutes. More water may be added if needed. Serve with honey and/or dried fruit and milk. 2 servings.

Seven-Grain Cereal (2 Servings)

Follow directions for and increase grain and water proportions in Seven-Grain Cereal to the following:

    1/3 cup whole wheat
    ¼ cup rye
    2 tablespoons millet
    2 tablespoons brown rice
    1 tablespoon flax seed
    3 tablespoons wheat germ
    2 tablespoons cornmeal (made by grinding dried corn in
        grinder or blender)
    3 to 4 cups water.

    4 servings.

**Whole Wheat Cereal
(Made in Thermos)**

A wonderful nutritious cereal that you make the night before.

    1½ cups hot water, actively boiling
    ½ cup cracked wheat

Place water and wheat in a 1-pint thermos bottle. Tightly cap and turn on its side. Leave overnight. In the morning, serve with milk and dried peaches, apples, raisins, dates, or prunes. 2 servings.

Whole Wheat Cereal
(Made in Crockpot)

1 cup water
½ cup cracked wheat

Place ingredients in crockpot before retiring. Turn crockpot on low. Cereal will be ready when you awaken. (If you prefer not to cook overnight, put ingredients in crockpot in the morning and cook on high for three hours.) Serve with milk and dried peaches, apples, raisins, dates, or prunes. 2 servings.

Wheat-Raisin Cereal

¾ cup whole wheat, cracked or ground
¾ cup raisins
2¼ cups water

Mix ingredients together in a saucepan. Bring to a boil. Turn heat down to a simmer and cook, stirring occasionally, until wheat is tender and thickened, about 8 to 10 minutes. More water may be added if needed. The raisins sweeten the cereal. Serve with milk or cream. 3 servings.

Sprouts-and-Fruit Breakfast

½ cup rye sprouts. Make by soaking 1/3 cup rye in water 12
    hours; drain and rinse with water twice a day. Let sprout
    12 to 48 hours.
¼ cup dried banana chips
Sliced dried pears
Sliced dried peaches
Raisins
Prunes
Sliced dried apples
Almonds
Sunflower seeds
Pumpkin seeds

For each serving: place ½ cup rye sprouts in a cereal dish. Top with ¼ cup dried bananas per serving. Serve lazy susan with assortment of remaining ingredients to be selected to sprinkle on top of sprouts and bananas. Serve with milk or cream. 1 serving.

Cornmeal Deluxe

    4 cups water
    1 cup cornmeal (make by grinding dried corn)
    ½ cup dried sliced pears, prunes, or raisins, if desired
    Melted unsalted butter or soymilk and honey

Bring water to a boil. Add cornmeal. Simmer, stirring constantly, until thick, about 10 to 12 minutes. Add dried fruit, if desired. Cover pan; turn off heat and let stand covered for 5 minutes. Serve by spoonfuls with butter or soymilk and honey. 6 servings.

Cornmeal Supreme

In Cornmeal Deluxe substitute ½ cup ground oats or seven-grain for ½ cup of the cornmeal. Make seven grain by grinding together equal parts of millet, rye, buckwheat, corn, wheat, barley, and brown rice.

Southern Spoon Bread

    1 cup yellow cornmeal (make by grinding or crushing
        dried corn in grinder or blender)
    2 cups cold water
    1 cup raw milk
    3 eggs, well beaten
    2 tablespoons unsalted melted butter
    ⅛ teaspoon freshly ground nutmeg

Combine cornmeal and water; boil 5 minutes, stirring constantly. Add to milk, eggs, butter and nutmeg; mix well. Pour in a well-greased 4½-by-8½-by-2½-inch loaf pan or 1½-quart baking dish. Bake at 400 degrees for 45 to 50 minutes. Serve from pan in which baked. To serve, spoon melted unsalted butter over Spoon Bread. Delicious served with ham. 6 servings.

COOKIES

Apple Cookies

A sweet change for your youngsters—cookies made from whole grain flour and honey

½ cup honey
½ cup apricot or soy oil
2 eggs
½ teaspoon vanilla
1 cup chopped or sliced dried apples, broken
2 cups freshly ground sifted whole wheat flour or 1½
    cups freshly ground sifted whole wheat flour and
    ½ cup freshly ground sifted millet flour
2 teaspoons baking powder
1½ teaspoons cinnamon
½ teaspoon allspice
½ cup chopped raisins
1 cup chopped walnuts

Mix honey and oil. Add eggs, vanilla and apples and mix well. Sift together flour, baking powder, cinnamon, and allspice. Add to first mixture, beating well. Stir in raisins and nuts. Drop by teaspoonfuls on a greased cookie sheet. Bake at 350 degrees about 15 minutes or until a toothpick inserted comes out clean. Yield: about 3 dozen cookies.

Special Oatmeal Cookies

¾ cup unsalted butter, apricot oil, or soy oil
¾ cup honey
1 egg
1 teaspoon vanilla
1 cup freshly ground sifted whole wheat flour
2 tablespoons bran
½ teaspoon baking soda
3 cups rolled oats
½ cup carob chips
1 cup chopped nuts
¾ cup chopped dried figs, apples,
    raisins, dates, bananas, or cherries

Cream together butter or oil, honey, egg, and vanilla. Sift together flour, bran, and soda and add to creamed mixture. Blend well. Stir in oats, carob chips, nuts, and dried fruit. Drop by teaspoonfuls on a greased cookie sheet. Bake at 350 degrees 12 to 15 minutes. Yield: about 5 dozen.

Persimmon Cookies

1 cup dried persimmon slices pureed in blender with 2/3 cup
    water (about 1 cup plulp)
1 teaspoon baking soda
½ cup unsalted butter
½ cup honey
1 egg
1 teaspoon lemon extract
2 tablespoons freshly grated lemon rind
2 cups freshly ground sifted whole wheat flour
1 teaspoon baking powder
½ teaspoon cinnamon
½ teaspoon freshly ground nutmeg
½ cup raisins
½ cup chopped nuts

Mix soda with persimmon; set aside. Beat together butter, honey, egg, lemon extract, and lemon rind. Add persimmon to egg mixture. Sift flour, baking powder, cinammon, and nutmeg together and add to pulp. Add nuts and raisins. Drop by spoonfuls on a greased, floured cookie sheet. Bake at 350 degrees 8 to 10 minutes. Yield: about 3 dozen cookies.

Persimmon-Oatmeal Drop Cookies

¾ cup unsalted butter
¾ cup honey
2 eggs
1 teaspoon vanilla
1 cup dried persimmon slices pureed in blender
    with 2/3 cup water (about 1 cup pulp)
1½ teaspoons baking soda
1½ cups freshly ground sifted whole wheat flour
2 teaspoons baking powder
½ teaspoon nutmeg
½ teaspoon cloves
1½ cups rolled oats
½ cup unsweetened coconut
½ cup nuts

Beat together butter, honey, eggs, and vanilla. Add soda to persimmon pulp, then add to first mixture. Sift together flour, baking powder, nutmeg, and cloves and add to persimmon mixture. Beat well. Mix in rolled oats, coconut, and nuts. Drop by spoonfuls on a greased, floured cookie sheet and bake at 375 degrees for about 12 minutes. Yield: 4 to 5 dozen cookies.

DESSERTS

Ambrosia

1 cup Cherry or Orange Yogurt
1 can (11 ounces) mandarin orange slices
1 can (8½ ounces) crushed pineapple
½ cup chopped pecans
2/3 cup coconut
Pomegranate seeds for garnish, if desired

Mix all ingredients together in a bowl. Garnish with pomegranate seeds or additional mandarin oranges and pineapple slices. 6 to 8 servings.

Apricot Delight

1 pound dried apricots
1 cup honey
1 tablespoon orange juice

½ tablespoon dried powdered orange rind or
   1 tablespoon freshly grated orange rind
½ teaspoon dried powdered lemon rind or 1 teaspoon
   freshly grated lemon rind
Pecans or blanched toasted almonds
Finely chopped unsweetened coconut, if desired

Grind apricots fine. Mix with honey, orange juice, and grated peels. Cook over low heat 10 minutes, stirring constantly. Cool slightly and drop by teaspoonful on greased cookie sheets. When cool, top each apricot confection with a pecan or blanched toasted almond. Roll in coconut, if desired. Yield: about 2½ dozen.

Fruit Compote

½ cup sliced dried bananas
½ cup sliced dried oranges without rind
½ cup sliced dried apples
½ cup sliced dried papaya, cantaloupe, honeydew,
   or watermelon
1 tablespoon fresh lemon juice
2 cups water
Whipped Cream Topping Made From Fruit Leather
Unsweetened coconut

Mix together first six ingredients, and place in refrigerator. Stir occasionally as fruit reconstitutes (10 or 20 minutes). Spoon into 6 glass dessert dishes. Top with Whipped Cream Topping Made From Fruit Leather. Strawberry, pineapple, or raspberry is a good combination. Sprinkle with coconut. 6 servings.

Fruit Cream Cheese Pinwheels

1 dried sheet of any of the following:
    Apricot Leather
    Apricot-Pineapple Leather
    Blueberry Leather
    Boysenberry Leather
    Cranberry Leather
    Grape Leather
    Peach Leather
    Pear-Cinnamon Leather
    Persimmon-Orange Leather
    Pink Pineapple Leather
    Plum Leather
    Pomegranate Leather
    Pumpkin Pie Leather
    Raspberry Leather
    Strawberry-Rhubarb Leather
    Strawberry Leather

2 tablespoons honey
½ teaspoon vanilla
1 cup Homemade Cream Cheese
1 or 2 tablespoons half and half or milk
¾ cup finely chopped walnuts or sunflower seeds

Add honey and vanilla to cream cheese and enough half and half or milk to soften. Spread evenly on one sheet of fruit leather; sprinkle with nuts or sunflower seeds. Beginning with 9-inch side, roll into a pinwheel. With a very sharp or electric knife, cut into ½- to ¾-inch slices. Arrange on plate or platter to serve. Yield: 12 to 18 pinwheels.

Walnut Pinwheels

1 dried sheet of any of the following fruit leathers:
    Apricot
    Boysenberry
    Cranberry-Orange
    Peach
    Pineapple-Banana
    Pumpkin
    Raspberry

Walnut halves
Toothpicks

Cut leather across in ¾-inch strips. Roll each strip around a walnut half and fasten with a toothpick. Yield: about 16 pinwheels.

New Orleans Strawberry Crepes

¾ cup freshly ground sifted whole wheat flour
½ teaspoon honey
2 eggs
½ cup plus 2 tablespoons milk or half and half
1¼ cups (2 recipes) Strawberry Jam
3 ounces (1/3 cup plus 1 teaspoon) Homemade Cream Cheese
¼ cup honey
1 teaspoon vanilla
1 cup whipping cream, whipped
Freshly grated nutmeg

Mix flour and ½ teaspoon honey. Blend in eggs. Add milk or half and half until batter is consistency of evaporated milk. Beat until smooth. Lightly oil a 6-inch frying pan with pastry brush dipped in oil. Heat pan. Pour 2 tablespoons batter at a time into pan, tilting quickly to distribute batter evenly. Cook until lightly browned, then turn over and brown on other side. Oil pan with brush and repeat until batter is completely used. Keep crepes warm in a towel.

Fill each crepe with about 2 tablespoons Strawberry Jam. Roll up crepes. Mix together cream cheese, ¼ cup honey, vanilla and whipped cream. Spoon over crepes. Sprinkle with nutmeg. 4 servings of 2 crepes each.

EGGS

Plain Omelet

½ cup powdered eggs
¼ cup water
¼ cup half and half (if camping, use water and add
    3 tablespoons nonfat dry milk, if desired)
⅛ teaspoon pepper
1 tablespoon unsalted butter, apricot oil or soy oil

Mix together first four ingredients in blender or by hand if camping. Melt butter or oil in 6- or 7-inch frying pan. Pour in egg mixture.

Cook slowly without turning until brown on the bottom. Fold over to serve. Serves 1 or 2.

Cheese-Tomato Omelet

    1 tablespoon dried parmesan cheese
    1 tablespoon chopped dried spinach
    1 tablespoon dried broken tomato slices
    ⅛ teaspoon dried powdered onion

Using the Plain Omelet recipe, sprinkle the above ingredients over egg mixture as it is browning in the frying pan.

Scrambled Eggs

Follow instructions for Plain Omelet recipe or Cheese-Tomato Omelet recipe. As egg mixture is cooking, keep stirring to make scrambled eggs.

FISH

Tuna Dip

    1 cup (1 recipe) Tuna Chip Snacks
    1/3 cup water
    2 tablespoons mayonnaise
    2/3 cup (6 ounces) Homemade Cream Cheese
    1 or 2 tablespoons cream or half and half

Puree first three ingredients together in blender until smooth. Add remaining ingredients. Blend until smooth. Serve as a dip with Whole Wheat Crackers. Yield: about 1 2/3 cups.

Tuna Spread

    1 cup (1 recipe) Tuna Chip Snacks
    1/3 cup water
    2 tablespoons mayonnaise

Puree all ingredients together in blender until smooth, scraping down sides with rubber scraper as needed. Yield: 2/3 cup Tuna Spread for crackers.

FROSTINGS AND TOPPINGS

Cream Cheese Frosting

  1 cup Homemade Cream Cheese
  2 tablespoons unsalted butter
  ¼ cup honey

Cream and beat all ingredients together. Spread evenly on Carrot Cake.

Whipped Cream and Honey Topping

  1 cup whipping cream, whipped
  2 tablespoons mild honey
  1 teaspoon vanilla

Mix all ingredients together. Yield: about 1½ cups.

Whipped Cream Topping Made from Fruit Leather

  ½ cup broken pieces of any flavor fruit leather,
      (one fruit leather removed from plastic wrap or parch-
      ment and torn into pieces will yield about ½ cup pieces)
  1/3 cup water
  1 cup whipping cream, whipped

Put pieces of fruit leather in blender. Add water and puree, pushing down mixture with rubber scraper until smooth and well blended. Gently fold fruit into whipped cream. Delicious served on desserts, pie, ice cream, salads (gelatin or fruit), pancakes, and waffles. Yield: about 2 cups.

HAM

Flavorful Ham Slice

  1 ham slice, cut 1 inch thick
  1 teaspoon prepared mustard
  2 tablespoons honey
  2/3 cup dried apricot halves pureed in blender with
      ½ cup water
  1 (number 1) can crushed unsweetened pineapple
  ¼ cup pineapple juice

Place ham slice in roasting pan. Mix mustard and honey and spread on top and sides of slice. Mix apricot puree, pineapple, and juice; pour over ham. Bake at 300 degrees 1½ hours. 4 to 6 servings.

ICE CREAM

Homemade Natural Vanilla Ice Cream

¾ cup evaporated milk
1 tablespoon unflavored gelatin softened in ½ cup water
½ cup honey
4 cups heavy or whipping cream, not whipped
2 cups half and half
2 teaspoons vanilla, if desired

Bring canned milk to a simmer over low heat. Add softened gelatine, stirring until dissolved. Cool. Add honey, cream, half and half, and vanilla, mixing until well blended. Proceed as in recipe for Homemade Natural Fruit Ice Cream. Yield: ½ gallon. You may add pureed dried fruit or fruit leather for variation of flavor.

Homemade Natural Fruit Ice Cream

    4 eggs
    1¼ cups honey
    3 cups milk
    4 cups cream or half and half
    1½ tablespoons vanilla
    4 cups dried strawberries, apricots, boysenberries,
        raspberries, peaches, or bananas pureed in blender
        with 3 cups milk

Beat eggs until light and fluffy. Add honey gradually and beat well. When the mixture becomes stiff and difficult to beat, add milk, cream, vanilla, and fruit mixture. Mix thoroughly. Pour into a gallon freezer; place lid on top. (Use 8 parts ice to 1 part salt for freezing.) Pack layers of crushed ice and coarse salt around gallon container in home freezer. Cover top of gallon container with crushed ice. Place towel on top of ice to rest knee or hand while turning crank or use electric home freezer. Unpack top layer of ice and check occasionally. Ice cream should have the consistency of thick pudding when finished. If not eaten immediately, replace cover and repack. (Use 4 parts ice to 1 part salt for packing). It will continue to harden and hold for several hours. Yield: about a gallon.

Apple Cinnamon Ice Cream

    1 cup sliced dried apple with or without peel and core
    1 cup water
    2 teaspoons fresh lemon juice
    ⅛ teaspoon cinnamon
    2 cups Homemade Natural Vanilla Ice Cream, softened

Puree apples, water, lemon juice, and cinnamon in blender until smooth. Use a rubber scraper to push down food in blender as it becomes a thick sauce. Taste for sweetness; if the apples used are Golden Delicious or another sweet variety, no honey will be needed. If apples are of a tart variety, it may be necessary to add honey to sweeten. Pour apple mixture over ice cream in a bowl and mix quickly. Place in freezing tray until ice cream becomes more firm, stirring if necessary. Yield: about 3 cups of ice cream.

Cherry Ice Cream

Substitute 1 cup pitted dried dark, sweet cherries for 1 cup sliced dried apples in Apple-Cinnamon Ice Cream.

Banana-Carob Yogurt Ice Cream

    1 cup dried banana chips
    1 cup raw milk
    1 cup (8 ounces) Homemade Yogurt
    2 to 4 tablespoons honey
    3 tablespoons carob powder

Blend dried bananas with milk in blender until smooth. Add remaining ingredients. Pour into freezing tray. Freeze until crystals form around edges. Stir. Freeze again until crystals form. Stir. Freeze until firm. Spoon into serving dishes. 4 servings.

Yummy Banana Yogurt Ice Cream

    1 cup dried banana chips
    1 cup raw milk
    1 cup (8 ounces) Homemade Yogurt
    2 to 4 tablespoons honey, if desired

Blend dried banana with milk in blender. Add yogurt and honey. Pour into freezing tray. Freeze until crystals form. Stir. Freeze again until crystals form. Stir. Freeze until firm. Spoon into serving dishes. 4 servings.

Yummy Banana Yogurt Ice Cream (without honey)

To make increase dried banana chips to 1¼ cups for added sweetness and omit honey.

Banana-Nut Ice Cream

    1 cup dried banana chips
    1 cup water
    ⅛ teaspoon cinnamon
    1 to 1½ tablespoons fresh lemon juice
    2 cups Homemade Natural Vanilla Ice Cream, softened
    ½ cup chopped walnuts

Puree banana chips, water, and cinnamon in blender until smooth. Use a rubber scraper to push down food in blender as it becomes a thick sauce. Taste for sweetness to determine whether 1 or 2 tablespoons lemon juice is needed. (The riper and sweeter the banana was when it was dried, the more lemon juice needed.) Pour banana mixture over ice cream and nuts in a bowl and mix quickly. Place in freezing tray until firm, stirring if necessary. Yield: about 3 cups of ice cream.

Blueberry Ice Cream

Substitute 1 cup dried blueberry halves for 1 cup dried bananas in Banana-Nut Ice Cream, omit nuts.

Pear Ice Cream

Substitute 1 cup sliced dried pears for 1 cup dried bananas in Banana-Nut Ice Cream; omit nuts, if desired.

Pineapple-Nut Ice Cream

Substitute 1 cup sliced dried pineapple for 1 cup dried bananas in Banana-Nut Ice Cream, omit lemon juice and cinnamon.

Cranberry-Orange Ice Cream from Cranberry-Orange Leather

½ cup broken pieces of Cranberry-Orange Fruit Leather; one fruit leather removed from plastic wrap or parchment paper and torn into pieces will yield about ½ cup pieces
½ cup water
1 to 1½ cups Homemade Natural Vanilla Ice Cream, softened

Puree Cranberry-Fruit Leather and water in blender until smooth. Pour over ice cream and mix quickly. Place in freezing tray until firm, stirring if necessary to prevent crystals from forming. Yield: about 1½ to 2 cups ice cream.

Fruit Ice Cream from Fruit Leather

In recipe for Cranberry Orange Ice Cream from Cranberry-Orange Leather, for ½ cup broken pieces Cranberry Fruit Leather substitute ½ cup broken pieces of any of the following:

Apple Leather made with Cherry, Strawberry, or Raspberry Juice
Apricot-Pineapple Leather
Banana-Coconut Leather
Banana-Peanut Butter Leather

Banana-Raspberry Leather
Blueberry-Banana Leather
Boysenberry Leather
Cherry-Banana Leather
Fruit Salad Leather
Grape Leather
Pineapple Leather
Pineapple-Banana Leather
Pink Pineapple Leather
Pomegranate Leather
Pumpkin Pie Leather
Raspberry Leather
Rosy Fruit Leather
Strawberry-Rhubarb Leather

Persimmon Ice Cream

1 cup sliced dried persimmon
1 cup water
¼ teaspoon cinnamon
⅛ teaspoon cloves
⅛ teaspoon mace
2½ tablespoons fresh lemon juice
2 cups Homemade Natural Vanilla Ice Cream, softened

Blend first five ingredients well in blender, pushing food down with rubber scraper as mixture becomes a thick sauce. Taste. Add lemon as needed because of sweetness of persimmon. Pour mixture over ice cream in a bowl and mix. Place in freezing tray until firm, stirring if necessary. Yield: about 3 cups.

Pumpkin-Nut Ice Cream

1 cup sliced dried pumpkin
1 cup water
¼ teaspoon cinnamon
⅛ teaspoon cloves
⅛ teaspoon mace
¼ cup honey
2 cups Homemade Natural Vanilla Ice Cream, softened
½ cup chopped nuts

Puree first six ingredients in blender until smooth. Use a rubber

scraper to push down food in blender as it becomes a thick sauce.
Pour pumpkin mixture over ice cream and nuts in a bowl and mix
quickly. Place in freezing tray until firm. Yield: about 3 cups.

Strawberry Ice Cream

    1 cup sliced dried strawberries
    1 cup water
    1 tablespoon fresh lemon juice
    Honey to taste
    2 cups Homemade Natural Vanilla Ice Cream, softened

Puree first three ingredients well in blender. Use rubber scraper
to push food down in blender as it becomes a thick sauce. Taste for
sweetness to determine amount of honey needed. Blend well. Pour
over ice cream in a bowl. Mix quickly. Place in freezing tray until
firm, stirring if necessary. Yield: about 3 cups.

Fruit Ice Cream

Substitute for 1 cup dried strawberries in Strawberry Ice Cream any dried fruit such as: apricots, peaches, boysenberries, raspberries, loganberries, oranges, tangerines, nectarines, cranberries, papaya.

Strawberry Ice Cream from Strawberry Leather

> ½ cup broken pieces of Strawberry Fruit Leather; one
>   fruit leather removed from plastic wrap or parchment
>   paper and torn into pieces will yield about ½ cup pieces
> ½ cup water
> 1½ to 2 cups Homemade Natural Vanilla Ice Cream, softened

Puree Strawberry Fruit Leather and water in blender until smooth. Pour over ice cream and mix quickly. Place in freezing tray until firm, stirring if necessary to prevent crystals from forming. Yield: about 1½ to 2 cups.

Watermelon Ice Cream

> 1 cup sliced dried watermelon
> 1 cup water
> 2 to 4 tablespoons fresh lemon juice
> 2 cups Homemade Natural Vanilla Ice Cream, softened

Puree watermelon with water in blender using a rubber scraper to push food down as it blends. Taste; add lemon juice to taste. Pour mixture over ice cream in a bowl and mix quickly. Place in freezing tray until firm, stirring if necessary. Yield: about 3 cups.

Fruit Yogurt Ice Cream

> 1¼ cup dried strawberries, boysenberries, raspberries, apricots,
>   peaches, or other favorite fruit
> 1 cup raw milk
> 1 cup (8 ounces) Homemade Yogurt
> 2 to 4 tablespoons honey, if desired

Blend dried fruit with milk in blender. Add yogurt and honey. Pour into freezing tray. Freeze until crystals form around edge. Stir. Freeze until firm. Spoon into serving dishes. 4 servings.

LAMB

Grecian Leg of Lamb

> 1 (5-pound) leg of lamb
> Freshly ground pepper
> 4 teaspoons dried powdered garlic
> ¼ cup unsalted butter
> 2 tablespoons fresh lemon juice
> ½ cup water
> 10 or 12 new red potatoes

Wash meat, dry, and place skin-side down on a rack in an open roasting pan. Season with pepper. Make 16 incisions in the meat and insert ¼ teaspoon garlic powder and ½ teaspoon butter in each incision. Insert meat thermometer in the thickest part of largest muscle; do not let thermometer rest in fat or on bone. Melt the remaining butter, mix with the lemon juice, and pour over meat. Add water to the bottom of the roasting pan. Bake at 350 degrees, allowing 30 minutes to the pound. For well-done lamb, the internal temperature is 175 to 180 degrees, for slightly rare or pink lamb, the internal temperature is 160 to 165 degrees. One hour before lamb is done, place potatoes in pan to cook and brown in drippings. Baked tomatoes can be added to roast 15 minutes before lamb is done or baked in a separate casserole. Serves 6.

Barbecued Lamb Riblets

3 pounds lamb riblets
1 medium onion, chopped
1½ tablespoons honey
2 tablespoons vinegar
1 cup dried powdered tomato mixed with ¼ cup water
1 cup dry white wine
⅛ teaspoon crushed pepper

Brown the lamb riblets on all sides. Pour off drippings. Mix together remaining ingredients and pour over riblets. Cover tightly and simmer slowly 1½ hours or until tender. Riblets can also be baked, covered, at 300 degrees for 1½ hours. Skim off fat that has accumulated on top of riblets. Serve with or over rice. 4 servings.

MAIN DISHES

Stuffed Cabbage Rolls

1 pound sausage (a hot spicy sausage is delicious)
1/3 cup chopped dried onion soaked in 1/3 cup water 30 minutes
1 pound ground beef
1 cup cooked rice
1 egg, beaten
1 large head of cabbage
1¼ cups sliced, dried powdered tomatoes mixed with 1¼ cups water
¼ teaspoon chili powder
¼ teaspoon dried crushed oregano
¼ cup dry sherry

Cook sausage in a heavy frying pan until sausage changes color. Pour off drippings. Cool. Mix together onion, ground beef, rice, and egg. Add cooked sausage to ground beef mixture. Mix together. Cut core from cabbage and carefully remove about 12 leaves so they do not break. Trim off hard parts. Drop 2 or 3 at a time in salted boiling water, cooking about 5 minutes to soften them. Divide meat mixture into about 12 parts. Place 1 part (a generous tablespoon) of the meat mixture on each cabbage leaf at the rib end. Start to roll, turning the sides of the leaf in, and make a neat cylinder. Fasten with wooden picks or tie with string. Arrange rolls in a baking dish. Mix together tomato mixture, chili powder, oregano, and wine. Pour over rolls. Cover and bake at 300 degrees for 1 hour. Makes about 12 cabbage rolls or 6 servings.

Devilishly Good Pizza

    1 pound Honey Whole Wheat Bread Dough—use ¼ of recipe
    ¾ cup dried powdered tomato mixed with ¾ cup water
    2 cloves garlic, minced
    ½ pound Mozzarella cheese, sliced thin
    ½ pound ground beef (or ½ cup broken pieces dried beef jerky)
    2 teaspoons dried oregano
    ½ teaspoon hot chili pepper
    Parmesan cheese

Cut dough in half. Pat and stretch each piece to fit lightly greased 12-inch pizza pans. Mix tomato sauce and garlic. Spread over dough. Arrange cheese on tomato mixture. Cook ground beef until it changes color; pour off drippings, or use beef jerky. Spoon over the two pizzas. Sprinkle with spices and Parmesan cheese. Do not let rise. Bake at 450 degrees for approximately 15 minutes or until browned and bubbly. Cut in wedges using kitchen shears. Serve hot. Yield: two 12-inch pizzas.

Easy Chili Casserole

An easy one-dish meal made with whole wheat. Omit beef jerky for a meatless meal.

    1 cup dried tomato slices, broken
    1 cup cracked wheat
    ¼ cup small broken pieces dried beef jerky, if desired
    ¼ cup chopped dried onion
    3 tablespoons chopped dried green pepper
    1 teaspoon chili powder
    1 teaspoon dried powdered garlic
    3½ cups water
    2 cups grated longhorn cheese
    Parsley, carrot sticks, and celery sticks, if desired

Mix first seven dry ingredients together. Add water and mix well. Pour into a greased 2-quart casserole. Bake at 350 degrees for 50 minutes. Top with grated cheese. Bake 10 minutes longer until cheese is melted and bubbling. If desired, garnish with parsley, carrot, and celery sticks. This makes 4 servings and is delicious with a vegetable or fruit salad.

PIE CRUSTS

Whole Wheat Pie Crust

1 cup freshly ground sifted whole wheat flour
3 tablespoons unsalted butter
2 tablespoons plus 2 teaspoons shortening
2 to 4 tablespoons cold water

Cut butter and shortening into flour using pastry blender until crumbs are about the size of small peas. Add cold water, a little at a time, mixing quickly and evenly through flour with fork until dough just holds in a ball. Use as little water as possible.

Roll to about ⅛ inch thickness between waxed paper or on pastry cloth. Line an 8- or 9-inch pie pan, allowing ½-inch crust to extend over edge. Fold edge under and crimp. For a baked pie shell, prick pastry with a fork and bake at 450 degrees 8 to 10 minutes. For a filled pie, do not prick crust; bake according to directions. *For a two-crust pie, double recipe.*

Sesame Seed Pie Crust

Sprinkle and press 2 tablespoons raw sesame seeds into a single unbaked Whole Wheat Pie Crust just before pricking pastry with a fork before baking.

Millet Whole Wheat Pie Crust

Substitute ¼ cup freshly ground millet flour for ¼ cup of the whole wheat flour in the recipe for Whole Wheat Pie Crust.

Seven-Grain Pie Crust

Substitute 1 cup freshly ground seven-grain flour for 1 cup whole wheat flour in the recipe for Whole Wheat Pie Crust. Make seven-grain flour by grinding together equal parts of the following grains: millet, rye, buckwheat, corn, wheat, barley, and oats.

PIES

Country Apple Pie

> 1¼ cups heavy cream (if unavailable, use whipping cream; do not whip)
> 2 tablespoons quick-cooking tapioca
> ½ cup honey
> ½ teaspoon freshly ground nutmeg
> ¼ teaspoon cinnamon
> 2 teaspoons lemon juice
> 2½ cups sliced dried apples
> Whole Wheat Pie Crust for 2-crust 9-inch pie
> 2 tablespoons unsalted butter

Mix first six ingredients together. In saucepan, heat to about 185 degrees (just under boiling). Add apples and toss. Pour half of apple mixture into pie shell. Dot with butter. Add remaining apple mixture. Using pastry brush, brush edge of crust with water. Put top crust on top of pie; cut air vents in top crust. Bake 350 degrees for 50 to 60 minutes, until apples are cooked and crust is lightly browned.

Strawberry or Apricot Whipped-Cream Cheese Pie

> 1 baked 8-inch Whole Wheat Pie Shell
> 3 ounces (1/3 cup plus 1 teaspoon) Homemade Cream Cheese
> ¼ cup honey
> 1 teaspoon vanilla
> 1 cup whipping cream, whipped
> 1¼ cups (2 recipes) Strawberry or Apricot Jam

Cream together cream cheese, honey, and vanilla. Fold in whipped cream. Pour whipped-cream mixture into pie shell, reserving a little for garnish. Spread strawberry or apricot jam on top of cheese mixture. Garnish with dollops of whipped cream mixture. Chill 3 or 4 hours before cutting to serve.

Fruit Whipped-Cream Cheese Pie

In the recipe for Strawberry or Apricot Whipped-Cream Cheese Pie, substitute 1¼ cups (2 recipes) of any of the following Fruit Jams for 1¼ cups Strawberry or Apricot Jam:

> Blackberry Jam
> Blueberry Jam

Boysenberry Jam
Cantaloupe Jam
Honeydew Melon Jam
Loganberry Jam
Nectarine Jam
Orange Jam
Papaya Jam
Peach Jam
Persimmon Jam
Pineapple Jam
Plum Jam
Raspberry Jam
Watermelon Jam

Pie from India

1 unbaked 8-inch Whole Wheat Pie Crust
2 eggs, separated
½ cup honey
1 teaspoon cinnamon
1 teaspoon ground cloves
½ cup pecan halves
½ cup raisins
1 tablespoon unsalted melted butter
1 tablespoon white vinegar
Homemade Natural Vanilla Ice Cream, whipped cream, or
    Orange Yogurt, if desired
Lemon leaves, if desired

Beat egg yolks until light and thick. Gradually add honey, cinnamon, and cloves. Add pecans, raisins, butter and vinegar. Gently fold in stiffly beaten egg whites (do not beat). Pour into an 8-inch unbaked pie shell. Bake at 400 degrees 30 minutes or until crust is done and topping is crisp and browned. Cool. Serve with vanilla ice cream, unsweetened whipped cream, or yogurt. Garnish with pecans. Arrange lemon leaves around pie for color. 6 servings.

Fruit Cobbler

3 cups sliced dried apples, peaches, or apricots, with
    or without peel, soaked in 3 cups warm water 1 or 2 hours
½ cup honey
¼ teaspoon dried lemon peel, powdered in blender,
    or ¼ teaspoon grated fresh lemon peel

½ cup unsalted butter
¾ cup freshly ground sifted whole wheat flour or ½ cup
    freshly ground sifted whole wheat flour plus ¼ freshly
    ground millet flour
2 teaspoons baking powder
¾ cup buttermilk
1 cup whipping cream, whipped
2 tablespoons honey
½ teaspoon vanilla

Mix together apples, honey, and lemon peel. Set aside. Place butter in a 2-quart casserole; heat in 325 degree oven until butter melts. Remove from oven. Sift flour with baking powder and mix with buttermilk. Pour batter in buttered casserole. Do not stir. Spoon fruit mixture on top of batter. Do not mix batter with fruit. Bake at 325 degrees 1 hour. Serve with whipped cream which has been mixed with honey and vanilla. 4 servings.

PORK

Apricot Pork Chops

6 rib or loin pork chops, ¾ inch thick
1 tablespoon apricot oil or soy oil
1 cup dried apricots soaked 1 or 2 hours or overnight
    in 1 cup water
2 tablespoons honey
1 tablespoon fresh lemon juice

Brown chops in oil. Pour off oil drippings. Arrange apricots on top of chops along with any liquid in which they were soaked. Add honey and lemon juice. Cover tightly and simmer 45 minutes or until tender. Arrange chops and apricots on platter. Spoon any sauce over chops. 6 servings.

Orange Glazed Pork Chops

6 rib or loin pork chops. ¾ to 1 inch thick
1 tablespoon apricot oil or soy oil
⅛ teaspoon pepper
1 tablespoon chopped dried onion
1/3 cup frozen concentrated orange juice, undiluted
¼ cup white raisins

Brown chops in oil. Pour off drippings. Season with pepper. Add remaining ingredients. Cover and simmer 45 minutes. Spoon raisin sauce over chops before serving. 6 servings.

Sweet-Sour Spareribs

Our favorite family recipe for ribs.

5 pounds (2 sides) pork spareribs, cut in serving-size pieces
3 tablespoons cornstarch or 1½ tablespoons arrowroot
1 tablespoon dry mustard
1 cup vinegar
¾ cup chopped or sliced dried pineapple reconstituted in
    ¾ cup water for 1 hour or 1 cup (No. 1 flat can) unsweetened
    crushed pineapple, undrained
2/3 cup honey
2/3 cup dried powdered tomato mixed with 2/3 cup water
¼ cup water
3 tablespoons chopped dried onion or dried broken onion pieces
    reconstituted in 3 tablespoons water for 20 minutes or
    1/3 cup finely chopped fresh onion
3 tablespoons soy sauce

Place ribs, meaty side up, in a single layer in large shallow pan. Brown at 425 degrees for 30 minutes; drain off fat. In a saucepan, mix cornstarch or arrowroot and mustard. Gradually stir in vinegar. Add remaining ingredients and cook over medium heat until thick and glossy, stirring constantly. Spoon about half of the sweet-sour sauce over the ribs. Reduce heat to 350 degrees and bake 45 minutes. Turn ribs; cover with remaining sauce. Bake 20 to 30 minutes longer or until done. Arrange on warm serving platter. 6 servings.

Spareribs with Apple-Raisin Stuffing

4 pounds spareribs (3 sides)
⅛ teaspoon pepper
Apple-Raisin Stuffing

Cut spareribs into pieces, approximately three ribs each. Season with pepper. Spread half the pieces with Apple-Raisin Stuffing. Cover with remaining sections of spareribs, turning rib ends down. Place spareribs on a rack in an open roasting pan and bake at 350 degrees for 1½ hours, or until meat is tender. 6 servings.

Apple-Raisin Stuffing

> 2 slices bacon
> 1/3 cup sliced dried celery soaked in 1/3 cup water 30 minutes
> 1/3 cup chopped dried onion, soaked 30 minutes in 1/3
>   cup water
> 3 cups sliced dried apples
> ½ cup raisins
> 2 cups coarse dry whole wheat bread crumbs
> 2 tablespoons dried snipped parsley
> ¼ cup milk
> ⅛ teaspoon pepper

Fry bacon until crisp. Remove from drippings and dice. Mix bacon with all remaining ingredients. Mix lightly. Yield: about 4½ cups stuffing.

POULTRY

Chicken Hawaiian

> 1 (2½ to 3-pound) frying chicken
> 1½ tablespoons cornstarch
> 1/3 cup honey
> 1 tablespoon fresh lemon juice
> ½ cup vinegar
> ½ cup soy sauce
> 1 teaspoon grated fresh ginger or ½ teaspoon powdered
>   ginger
> ¼ teaspoon dried powdered garlic
> ½ cup pineapple juice
> ½ cup dried sliced pineapple cubes
> ½ cup papaya cubes, watermelon cubes, or canned
>   mandarin oranges, drained

Cut chicken into serving pieces. Mix together cornstarch and honey. Add lemon juice, vinegar, soy sauce, ginger, garlic, and pineapple juice. Pour marinade over chicken in shallow (9-by-9-inch or 8-by-12-inch) aluminum-foil-lined baking dish. Add pineapple cubes. Bake uncovered at 350 degrees 1 hour, basting occasionally. Add papaya, watermelon, or mandarin oranges; baste and bake 10 minutes longer. Serve with a bowl of cooked rice or over rice. Garnish with watercress. If desired, toast ¼ cup shaved almonds and 1 tablespoon butter in a shallow pan at 350 degrees until almonds are lightly browned (5 to 10 minutes); sprinkle over chicken. Yield: 4 servings.

Chicken Luau

If you want to have this for a church group, the amounts given are for 6 as well as 24 people.

For 6
- 1 (3-pound) chicken
- 1 quart water
- 3 tablespoons cornstarch
- Pepper to taste
- 2 cups cooked rice
- 1 can (5½ ounces) chow mein noodles
- ¾ cup flake coconut
- ¾ cup sliced dried celery
    - soaked 30 minutes in
    - ¾ cup water
- ¾ cup sliced dried onion
    - soaked 30 minutes in
    - ¾ cup water
- 6 slices pineapple
- 18 slices dried tomatoes
    - reconstituted by placing
    - slices on a tray with
    - a little water on top
    - of each and refrigerating
    - 10 or 20 minutes
- ¾ parmesan cheese
- ¾ cup toasted slivered almonds
- 1 bottle (5 ounces) soy sauce

For 24
- 4 (3-pound) chickens
- 4 quarts water
- ¾ cup cornstarch
- Pepper to taste
- 8 cups cooked rice
- 5 cans (5½-ounce) chow mein noodles
- 3 cups flake coconut
- 3 cups dried celery soaked 30 minutes in 3 cups water
- 3 cups dried onion soaked 30 minutes in 3 cups water
- 24 (3 large cans) slices pineapple
- 72 slices dried tomatoes
- 3 cups (1 8-ounce can) Parmesan cheese
- 3 cups (10 ounces) toasted slivered almonds
- 1 large bottle (12 ounces) soy sauce

Cook each chicken, covered, in 1 quart water about 1 hour or until done. Cool. Remove meat from and discard bones; add enough water to make 3 cups per chicken. Thicken by adding some of liquid to cornstarch to make a paste. Then add paste to chicken liquid and cook until thick and clear; season with pepper to taste.

To serve, arrange on each plate about 1/3 cup rice in center surrounded by a ring of chow mein noodles. Top rice with a heaping tablespoon of coconut, about ½ cup of chicken and gravy, 2 tablespoons celery, and 2 tablespoons onion. On top of this layer, 1 pineapple slice and 3 tomato slices. Add 1 heaping tablespoon Parmesan cheese and 1 heaping tablespoon almonds. Sprinkle generously with soy sauce.

For a large number, set up service on an assembly-line basis. Do not let guests serve themselves as they tend to leave out some of the layers which make this entree delicious and unique.

Yellow Rice and Chicken Casserole
(Paella)

> ½ teaspoon garlic powder
> ¼ cup chopped dried onion soaked in ½ cup hot water
>   20 to 30 minutes
> ¼ cup olive oil or 2 tablespoons unsalted butter with
>   2 tablespoons apricot oil or soy oil
> 1 frying chicken, quartered
> 1¼ cups dried broken tomato slices soaked 10 minutes
>   in 1½ cups hot water
> 2 chicken bouillon cubes
> 4 cups water
> 1 teaspoon ground saffron
> 1 dried bay leaf, crushed
> 1 cup uncooked rice
> 2 green peppers cut in ½-inch strips
> ½ cup dried green peas soaked in 1 cup hot water
>   overnight and cooked covered until tender, adding
>   more water if needed

Cook garlic and onion in olive oil or butter with oil until onion is transparent. Remove and reserve for later use. Fry chicken until lightly browned. Add onions, garlic, tomatoes, bouillon cubes, and water. Bring to a boil and cook 5 minutes. Add remaining ingredients except peas. Stir thoroughly and place in a 3½- or 4-quart covered casserole. Bake 350 degrees for 20 minutes. Serve garnished with small green peas. Serves 4.

Turkey or Chicken Chop Suey

> 1 pound uncooked turkey or chicken breast, cut in ¾-inch cubes
> 1 tablespoon apricot oil, soy oil, or unsalted butter
> 3 vegetable bouillon cubes
> 3 chicken bouillon cubes
> ½ cup unsweetened pineapple juice
> 2 tablespoons soy sauce
> ½ teaspoon ginger
> ½ teaspoon horseradish
> ½ cup sliced dried celery soaked 30 minutes in ½ cup
>   warm water
> ½ cup sliced dried green pepper soaked 30 minutes in
>   ½ cup warm water
> ½ cup whole or sliced dried mushrooms

½ cup dried tomato slices, broken
¼ cup chopped dried onions
¼ cup dried zucchini slices
1½ cups (5 ounces) fresh Chinese pea pods
2 cups (¼ pound) fresh bean sprouts

Quickly panfry turkey in oil or butter. Cook on high heat 3 or 4 minutes. Remove from heat and set aside in covered pan to keep warm. In another pan, dissolve and crush bouillon cubes in pineapple juice and soy sauce. Add ginger, horseradish, and all vegetables except bean sprouts. Simmer 2 minutes. Add turkey. Serve immediately over a bed of fresh bean sprouts. 4 servings.

Turkey with Apricot Stuffing

1 (6- to 8-pound) turkey
¼ cup chopped dried celery
¼ cup chopped dried onion
½ cup unsalted butter, melted
1 package (6½ ounces) prepared cornbread stuffing
½ cup broth from turkey giblets or milk, or a combination
    of both
1 can (6 ounces) water chestnuts, drained and thinly sliced
½ cup dried apricots

Wash turkey and pat dry. Simmer giblets and neck in water to cover until tender, 1½ to 2 hours; do not add liver until last 45 minutes. Remove meat from neck and dice giblets. Season with pepper. Reserve liquid.

Cook celery and onions in part of butter until vegetables are cooked but not browned. Add, with remaining butter, to cornbread stuffing mix. Mix in broth or milk and broth, water chestnuts, dried apricots, giblets and neck meat. Stuff neck and body cavity of turkey lightly. Truss openings. Tie or place wings and legs close to body. Place turkey on rack in roasting pan. Brush with additional butter. Bake at 325 degrees, allowing 25 minutes per pound for a 6- to 8-pound bird or 20 minutes per pound for a larger bird, or until meat thermometer inserted in breast or thigh reaches the internal temperature of 185 degrees. For a large bird, double stuffing ingredients, allowing about ½ to ¾ cup stuffing per pound. Any remaining stuffing can be baked in a greased casserole during last 45 minutes of baking time.

For a firmer, more easily carved bird, allow it to stand 20 minutes before carving.

Peach Garnish for Turkey

Use firm canned peach halves. Put about 1 teaspoon each of butter, brandy, and ½ teaspoon honey in each half. Place halves on rack with turkey or in buttered casserole during last 15 minutes of baking time. Fill peach halves with tiny sprigs of watercress or parsley. Garnish turkey with peach halves.

SALADS

Bean Sprout Salad

> 1/3 cup French dressing
> ¼ cup Homemade Yogurt
> 1 tablespoon soy sauce
> 1 pound fresh or 1½ cups dried bean sprouts soaked 10 to
>   20 minutes in 3 cups hot water
> ¼ cup grated dried beets soaked 10 minutes in ½ cup hot water
> 4 green onions and part of tops, thinly sliced diagonally
> 2 tablespoons chopped pimento
> Tomato slices
> Watercress
> 2 tablespoons unsalted butter
> ¼ cup sesame seeds

Mix French dressing, yogurt, and soy sauce together. Chill thoroughly. Combine bean sprouts, beets, onions, and pimiento. Chill thoroughly. Toss chilled dressing and ice-cold vegetables in chilled serving bowl. Garnish with tomato slices and watercress. Saute sesame seeds 2 or 3 minutes in butter, stirring constantly, until mixture is hot, bubbly and seeds are lightly browned. Pour sizzling mixture over icy salad. Serve immediately. Guests enjoy the temperature contrast of the hot seeds over cold vegetables as well as the lovely flavor of the salad. 4 to 6 servings.

Swiss Cabbage Salad

> 2 cups shredded dried cabbage
> 1 cup half and half
> 2 teaspoons honey
> 2 teaspoons vinegar
> Pinch of pepper
> 2 green onions, thinly sliced

Place cabbage in a high-walled container. Mix together half and half, honey, vinegar, and pepper; pour over cabbage. Let soak 10 to 20 minutes refrigerated or at room temperature. Sprinkle with onion. About 6 servings.

Pineapple-Cabbage Slaw

> 1 cup shredded dried cabbage soaked 10 minutes in 2/3 cup
>   warm water and chilled
> ½ cup Pineapple Yogurt
> ½ cup Raw Peanuts

Mix cabbage with yogurt. Toss with nuts. 3 to 4 servings.

Carrot Salad

> 2 cups grated dried carrots, soaked about five minutes
>   in 2 cups warm water
> 1 cup drained, crushed, unsweetened pineapple
> 1 cup raisins
> ½ cup chopped walnuts
> ¼ cup salad dressing or mayonnaise
> 2 tablespoons unsweetened pineapple juice
> 12 to 16 lettuce cups, if desired
> 1 tablespoon chopped dried spinach leaves

Mix carrots, pineapple, raisins, and walnuts. Chill. Blend salad dressing or mayonnaise and pineapple juice; pour over carrot mixture. Toss and arrange in lettuce cups. Sprinkle with spinach leaves. Yield: 12 to 14 servings.

Carrot-Pineapple Slaw

> 1 cup grated dried carrots soaked 10 minutes in 2/3 cup
>   warm water and chilled
> 1 cup shredded dried cabbage soaked in 2/3 cup warm water
>   and chilled
> 1 cup Pineapple Yogurt
> 1 cup raw peanuts or chopped raw nuts

Toss together carrots, cabbage, yogurt, and nuts. 6 to 8 servings.

Cucumber-Tomato Salad

1 cup peeled dried cucumbers
1 cup sliced dried tomatoes
¼ cup vinegar
¼ cup oil
6 to 8 lettuce cups
2 tablespoons chopped fresh onion
2 tablespoons chopped fresh parsley

Place cucumbers and tomatoes in a high-walled container. Pour vinegar and oil over vegetables. Let stand 10 to 20 minutes at room temperature or in the refrigerator. Arrange in lettuce cups. Sprinkle with onion and parsley. 6 to 8 servings.

German Cucumber Salad

2 cups sliced and peeled dried cucumber
½ cup half and half
1 teaspoon honey
1 teaspoon vinegar
Pinch of pepper
1 green onion, thinly sliced
1 teaspoon dried crushed parsley

Place cucumbers in a high-walled container. Mix together half and half, honey, vinegar, and pepper; pour over cucumbers. Let soak 10 to 20 minutes refrigerated or at room temperature. Sprinkle with onions and dried parsley. Cucumbers will be limp, but fresh and tasty. About 6 servings.

SAUCES

Fresh Applesauce

This applesauce will taste fresher than any you have ever eaten. Since it is not cooked it retains most of its flavor and nutrition.

1½ cups sliced dried apple with or without peel and core
1½ cups water
1½ teaspoons fresh lemon juice
⅛ to ¼ teaspoon cinnamon
Pinch freshly ground nutmeg
Honey to taste, if desired

Puree all ingredients except honey in blender, pushing down food with rubber scraper until smooth and blended. Taste for sweetness; if apples used are Golden Delicious or another sweet variety, no honey will be needed. If apples are of a tart variety, it may be necessary to add honey to sweeten. Yield: about 1½ cups. Double recipe for larger amount.

Fresh Pear Sauce

Substitute 1½ cups dried sliced pear, with or without seeds and core, for apples in Fresh Applesauce. Omit honey, as pears are normally sweet enough without it.

Fruit Sauce from Fruit Leather

    1 cup broken pieces of any flavor fruit leather, two fruit
       leathers removed from plastic wrap or parchment and torn
       into pieces will yield about 1 cup of pieces
    1 cup water

Put pieces of fruit leather in blender. Add water and puree, pushing down mixture with rubber scraper as necessary to make sauce or until smooth and well blended. Serve over ice cream, pudding, fresh fruit salads, desserts, pancakes and waffles. Yield: about 1¼ cups.

Creamy Horseradish Sauce

    ½ cup whipping cream, whipped
    2 tablespoons grated dried horseradish
    ⅛ teaspoon honey
    2 tablespoons plain commercial yogurt

Fold ingredients together. Serve cold with roast beef. Yield: about 1¼ cups. 4 to 6 servings.

SNACKS

Banana Peanut Butter Snacks

    Dried Banana Chips
    Peanut butter

Put a small dab of peanut butter on a banana chip. Top with another banana chip. Make as many as desired.

Raisin Peanut Snack

> 2/3 cup raw peanuts which have been dried overnight
>   (8 to 12 hours) at 118 degrees in the dehydrator
> 1/3 cup Homemade Raisins

Mix together and serve as a snack. Yield: 1 cup.

SOUPS

A Cup of Soup
(Split Pea)

> 3 tablespoons dried peas
> 1 chicken bouillon cube
> ¾ cup hot water
> ¼ teaspoon dried powdered onion
> ⅛ teaspoon freshly ground black pepper
> ¼ cup half and half or water
> ¼ cup julienne strips ham, if desired

Powder dried peas in blender until fine like flour. It may be necessary to stop blender from time to time and, using a rubber scraper, mix powdered peas which drop to the bottom of the blender with the other more coarsely ground ones on top. Yield: about 3 tablespoons powdered peas. Set aside. Dissolve bouillon cubes in ¾ cup hot water. Add onion powder, black pepper, and ¼ cup half and half or water. Heat almost to boiling. Add powdered peas and ham. Serve immediately. Yield: about 1 cup.

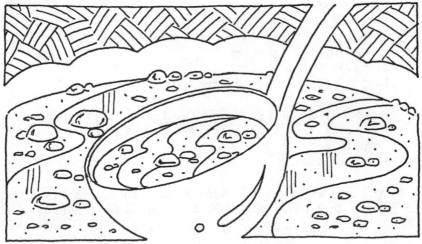

Asparagus Soup

Substitute 3 tablespoons dried powdered asparagus for 3 table-spoons dried powdered peas in A Cup of Soup.

Appetizer Beer-and-Cheese Soup

    ¼ cup grated dried carrot, soaked 10 to 20 minutes in ¼
        cup warm water
    1 teaspoon dried minced or powdered onion
    2 tablespoons unsalted butter
    1 chicken bouillon cube
    ¾ cup milk
    ¾ cup (packed) grated cheese (half sharp Cheddar and
        half mild Cheddar), measured after grating
    2 tablespoons freshly ground whole wheat flour
    ¼ to 1/3 cup cream or half and half
    ½ can beer (¾ to 1 cup)
    ⅛ teaspoon white pepper

Saute carrot and onion in butter until carrot is tender; add bouil-lon cube and dissolve. Add milk and heat. Mix cheese and flour and add to first mixture slowly, stirring until dissolved. Add cream. At this point soup can be left covered until serving time. Before serving add beer and pepper and heat but do not boil. Yield: 4 cups.

Corn-Tomato Chowder

    3 cups water
    1 cup coarsely cracked wheat
    1 cup dried corn soaked 1 hour in 2 cups warm water
    ¼ cup chopped dried onion
    2 tablespoons apricot or soy oil
    1 cup dried tomato slices, broken and soaked 1 hour in 1
        cup water
    ½ cup dried chopped green pepper soaked 1 hour in ½ cup water
    ½ cup broken pieces beef jerky (Favorite Beef Jerky)
    3 cups milk
    3 cups half and half

Bring 3 cups water to a boil. Add wheat and corn. Simmer, covered, 15 minutes. In a frying pan, saute onion in oil for 3 minutes. Add tomato, green pepper, and jerky. Steam, covered, 15 minutes. Add to first mixture along with milk and half and half. Heat thoroughly. Serve immediately. Serves six.

Chilled Cucumber Soup (Appetizer)

> ¼ cup dried, powdered cucumber (powder about 2/3
>   cup very dry cucumber slices, with or without peel,
>   in blender)
> 2 cups buttermilk
> 1 chicken bouillon cube
> 1 teaspoon dried powdered green pepper, if desired
> ⅛ teaspoon freshly ground black pepper
> ⅛ teaspoon dried powdered onion

Blend cucumber and about ½ cup buttermilk in blender. Add bouillon cube and blend until cube is dissolved. Blend in remaining buttermilk and remaining ingredients. Serve chilled or with crushed ice. Yield: 2 cups.

Cream of Spinach Soup

> 2 tablespoons unsalted butter
> 1 teaspoon onion powder
> ¼ teaspoon freshly grated nutmeg
> 2 chicken bouillon cubes
> 1½ cups raw milk
> ½ cup half and half
> ¼ cup dried powdered spinach

Melt butter in saucepan. Add onion powder, nutmeg and bouillon cubes. Crush and dissolve bouillon cubes adding a little milk if necessary. Add remaining milk and half and half. Heat to 185 degrees (just below boiling). Place spinach powder in blender. Pour hot milk mixture over spinach. Blend well. Serve at once. Yield: 3 small cups of soup as an appetizer or 1 large bowl (2 cups) as a main entree.

Cream of Asparagus Soup

Substitute ¼ cup dried powdered asparagus for ¼ cup dried powdered spinach in Cream of Spinach Soup.

Cream of Broccoli Soup

Substitute ¼ cup dried powdered broccoli for ¼ cup dried powdered spinach in Cream of Spinach Soup.

Cream of Cabbage Soup

Substitute ¾ cup dried shredded cabbage for ¼ cup dried powdered spinach in Cream of Spinach Soup. Do not powder dried cabbage in blender, just add it to the hot milk mixture.

Cream of Carrot Soup

Substitute ¼ cup dried powdered carrots for ¼ cup dried powdered spinach in Cream of Spinach Soup.

Cream of Celery Soup

Substitute ¼ cup dried powdered celery for ¼ cup dried powdered spinach in Cream of Spinach Soup.

Cream of Green Bean Soup

Substitute ½ cup dried powdered mushrooms for ¼ cup dried powdered spinach in Cream of Spinach Soup.

Cream of Mushroom Soup

Substitute ½ cup dried powdered mushrooms for ¼ cup dried powdered spinach in Cream of Spinach Soup.

Cream of Swiss Chard Soup

Substitute ¾ cup dried shredded swiss chard for ¼ cup dried powdered spinach in Cream of Spinach Soup. Do no powder dried swiss chard in blender, just add it to the hot milk mixture.

Cream of Tomato Soup

Substitute ¼ cup dried tomato powder for ¼ cup dried powdered spinach in Cream of Spinach Soup.

Easy Tomato Soup

    1 cup dried powdered tomato
    6 to 8 cups water
    1 cup nonfat dry milk powder
    ⅛ teaspoon pepper
    1 teaspoon dried crushed parsley

Mix tomato powder, 3 cups water, milk powder and pepper in blender. Add remaining water and heat to serve. Sprinkle with parsley. 6 to 8 servings.

Tomato Beef Soup

    1 cup dried powdered tomato
    6 to 8 cups beef broth, bouillon, or consomme
    ⅛ teaspoon pepper
    6 to 8 wedges lemon or lime, if desired

Mix tomato powder, 3 cups liquid, and pepper in blender. Add remaining water. Heat to serve, if desired. If made with bouillon or consomme, soup can also be served cold. Serve with lemon or lime wedges.

Tomato Rice Soup

To hot Tomato Beef Soup, add ½ cup rice. Cover and simmer until rice is tender. Omit lemon or lime wedges. 6 to 8 servings.

Swedish Fruit Soup

    ½ cup dried cranberry halves
    2 quarts (8 cups) apple juice
    1 pound dried fruit (half apricots and half prunes)
    ½ cup raisins
    ½ orange rind, cut in pieces
    2-inch stick cinnamon
    4 medium apples, peeled and sliced
    ¼ cup quick-cooking tapioca

Puree dried cranberries with ½ cup apple juice in blender. Add to remaining apple juice and combine with all ingredients in a large kettle. Bring to a boil. Reduce heat and simmer 30 minutes, stirring often. Cook until fruit is tender and liquid is slightly thickened and clear. Serve hot or cold as a dessert. The Swedish serve it hot on Christmas Eve, and cold on Christmas morning. Scandinavians consider it healthful and traditionally serve it to expectant mothers. 10 to 12 servings.

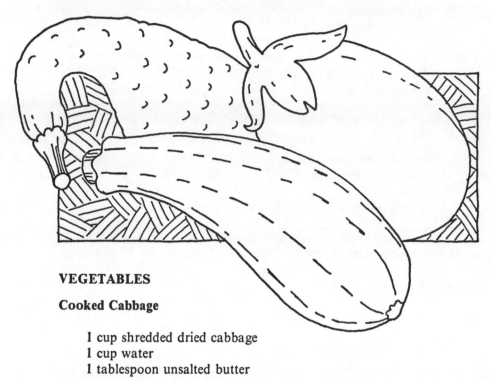

VEGETABLES

Cooked Cabbage

> 1 cup shredded dried cabbage
> 1 cup water
> 1 tablespoon unsalted butter

Soak cabbage in water in high-walled container 15 to 20 minutes. Simmer 3 to 5 minutes until tender. Add butter. About 4 servings.

Eggplant Grain Pilaf

> ½ cup hulled millet
> ½ cup whole wheat grain or buckwheat groats
> 4 cups lukewarm water
> 1 cup dried broken small pieces eggplant, with or without peel
> 2/3 cup (about 10 slices) dried broken small pieces apple, with
>   or without peel and core
> 3 tablespoons dried, chopped onion
> 1 teaspoon dried crushed oregano

Place millet and wheat or buckwheat groats in a 1½-quart oven-proof casserole. Add water. Cover and soak 4 hours or overnight. Add remaining ingredients, mixing well. Place a round rack in a large pan or kettle with casserole and its contents (including water in which grain was soaked) on top of rack. Add water to pan or kettle until it touches bottom of casserole. Leave casserole uncovered, but cover large pan or kettle. Turn heat on high until water in pan is boiling; reduce heat to simmer so that water steams. Steam 30 minutes. Remove pilaf from heat; stir well. Serve hot with unsalted butter or home-made yogurt. 6 to 8 servings. Pilaf may be kept hot 15 or 20 minutes in closed steamer pan with heat off.

Creamed Spinach

4 cups chopped dried spinach
1½ tablespoons unsalted butter
1½ tablespoons freshly ground whole wheat flour
1 cup milk
1½ cups half and half
1 teaspoon dried powdered onion
¼ teaspoon fresh grated nutmeg
⅛ teaspoon freshly ground pepper

Pour hot water through spinach in a colander; set aside. Melt butter in saucepan. Add flour, stirring constantly; gradually add milk. Cook until thickened. Add remaining ingredients and spinach. Heat through 4 servings.

Spinach-Cheese Pie

6 cups chopped dried spinach
2 cans (10½ ounces) cream of mushroom soup, undiluted
4 eggs, beaten
Soy oil or apricot oil
½ cup Parmesan cheese

To reconstitute spinach, pour hot water through spinach in a colander. Mix together spinach, soup, and eggs. Oil a 10-inch pie plate well; sprinkle oiled plate with ¼ cup Parmesan cheese. Pour in spinach mixture; sprinkle top of spinach mixture with remaining ¼ cup Parmesan cheese. Bake 375 degrees about 1¼ hours or until sharp knife inserted in custard comes out clean. Cut in wedges to serve. 10 to 12 servings.

Colorful Zucchini

    2 tablespoons unsalted butter
    1½ cups sliced dried zucchini reconstituted in 1½ cups
        hot water for 10 or 15 minutes, drained
    2/3 cup grated cheddar cheese
    ½ cup coarsely chopped raw almonds
    3 tablespoons dried broken tomato slices or ½ cup
        cherry tomatoes cut in half

Melt butter in frying pan. Arrange zucchini in a layer. Sprinkle with cheese, almonds, and tomatoes. Cover tightly. Heat 2 to 3 minutes or until cheese melts and dish is hot. 4 servings.

Western Yellow Neck Squash

    2 tablespoons butter
    3 tablespoons chopped fresh onion
    1½ cups sliced dried yellow neck squash reconstituted
        in 1½ cups hot water for 10 to 15 minutes, drained
    2/3 cup grated cheddar cheese
    1/3 cup cooked crumbled bacon
    1 tablespoon dried crushed spinach, if desired

Cook onions in butter in frying pan slightly. Turn off heat. Arrange squash in a layer. Sprinkle with cheese, bacon, and spinach. Cover tightly. Heat 2 to 3 minutes or until cheese melts and dish is hot. 4 servings.

YOGURT

Apple or Pear Yogurt

> 1 1/3 cups dried apple or pear pureed in blender with 1
>   cup water
> 2 cups Homemade Yogurt
> Honey to taste (2 or 3 tablespoons)
> ⅛ teaspoon cinnamon

Mix fruit and yogurt together. Add honey and cinnamon. Refrigerate. Yield: 3 cups yogurt.

Cherry or Orange Yogurt

> 1 1/3 cups pitted dried cherries or sliced dried orange
>   without peel, pureed in blender with 1 cup water
> 2 cups Homemade Yogurt
> Honey to taste (2 or 3 tablespoons)

Mix fruit and yogurt together. Add honey and cinnamon. Refrigerate. Yield: 3 cups yogurt.

Pineapple Yogurt

> 2/3 cup fresh pineapple or unsweetened, drained,
>   crushed pineapple
> 1 cup Homemade Yogurt
> Honey to taste (1 or 2 tablespoons)

Puree pineapple in blender. Mix with yogurt and honey. Refrigerate. Yield: about 1½ cups yogurt.

Fresh Fruit Yogurt

> 1 cup pureed fresh strawberries, peaches, boysenberries,
>   blueberries, apricots, persimmon, raspberries, oranges,
>   or bananas
> 1 cup Homemade Yogurt
> Honey to taste

Mix all ingredients together. Refrigerate. Yield: 2 cups yogurt.

Fruit-Flavored Yogurt

> 2/3 cup dried fruit such as bananas, apples, apricot
>   peaches, raspberries, boysenberries, or strawberries,
>   pureed in blender with ½ cup water
> 1 cup Homemade Yogurt
> Honey, to taste (1 to 2 tablespoons)

Mix together fruit puree and yogurt. Add honey to taste. Refrigerate. Yield: 1½ cups yogurt.

Tomato Yogurt

> 1 cup Homemade Yogurt
> 3 tablespoons dried tomato powder

Mix together until tomato is blended. Refrigerate. Yield: 1 cup yogurt.

MISCELLANEOUS

Reconstituted Fruit for Breakfast, Dessert, Salad, or Side Dish

The fruit is not stewed or cooked at all. It has a much fresher flavor and is more nutritious this way.

> 1 cup dried fruit such as apricots, strawberries,
>   dark sweet cherries, blueberries, boysenberries,
>   raisins, prunes, apples, raspberries, pears
> 1 cup water
> Fresh lemon juice, if desired
> Honey, if desired

Soak fruit in 1 cup water, in a high-walled container so that water covers fruit 1 or 2 hours or overnight in refrigerator. Taste the fruit. It may taste wonderful just as it is, but if it is too sweet, add a little lemon juice; if it is too sour, add a little honey. (The sweetness of fruit varies.) If you do not cook or stew it, it will taste very fresh. Yield: about 1 cup of fruit. 2 servings for breakfast, dessert, salad, or a side dish.

Fresh Tomato Catsup

> 1 cup dried, powdered tomato

1 to 1¼ cups water
½ to 1 teaspoon chopped hot pepper (fresh or hot
   pepper flakes), if desired
3 tablespoons chopped onions
½ teaspoon dried crushed oregano, if desired

Puree all ingredients together in blender, adding enough water to make consistency of catsup. Serve over a sandwich meat or eggs. Yield: 1¼ to 1½ cups catsup (10 to 12 ounces).

Tomato Paste

1 cup dried powdered tomato
1¼ cups water

Mix together in blender. Yield: about 1½ cups (12 ounces).

Tomato Sauce

1 cup dried powdered tomato
1¾ cups water

Mix together in blender. Yield: about 2 cups (16 ounces).

Salt Substitute

If you have arthritis or high blood pressure, you may wish to try this one.

1 tablespoon mustard seed
3 tablespoons dried powdered tomato
3 tablespoons dried ground or powdered stems and bulbs
   from dried seaweed

Powder mustard seed in blender or grinder. Add remaining ingredients and blend well. Use instead of salt.

Appendix 1: Dehydration vs. Canning and Freezing

Preservation type and amount	gm. protein	mg. calcium	Total gm. carb. & fiber	mg. vit. C	mg. iron
Half can 100 gm. apricots					
canned in syrup	.6	11	.4	−4	0.3
dehydrated	5.6	86	.8	15	5.3
frozen, sweet	.7	10	.6	20	.9
100 gm. peaches					
canned in syrup	1.8	18	91.2	13	1.4
dehydrated	21.8	81	399.2	63	15.9
frozen, sweet	1.8	18	102.5	50	2.3
100 gm. peas					
canned	15	––	56	40	7.7
dehydrated	109	––	273	20	23.1
frozen	24	––	58	60	9.1
100 gm. carrots					
canned	2.7	––	113	2	3.2
dehydrated	3.8	––	367	15	27.2
frozen	29.9	––	115	4	4.9

Preservation type and amount	mg. phosphate	I.U. vit. A	mg. potassium	mg. ribr.	mg. niacin
Half can 100 gm. apricots					
canned in syrup	15	1,740	234	.03	0.4
dehydrated	139	14,100	1,260	.10	3.6
frozen, sweet	19	1,680	229	.04	1.0
100 gm. peaches					
canned in syrup	54	1,950	590	.11	2.5
dehydrated	685	22,680	22,680	.43	35.2
frozen, sweet	59	2,950	562	.18	.18
100 gm. peas					
canned	––	2,040	––	––	––
dehydrated	––	4,010	––	––	––
frozen	––	3,020	––	––	––
100 gm. carrots					
canned	––	45,360	––	––	––
dehydrated	––	453,600	––	––	––
frozen	––	49,200	––	––	––

*Analysis charts, U.S. Department of Agriculture Research

Appendix 2: What Will You Be Eating Today?

The following menu is translated into the preservatives and additives likely to be contained in the very foods you may be eating today. Here is what you could be eating for lunch or dinner:

Juice—Benzoic Acid (preservative)
Dimethyl polysiloxane (anti-foaming agent)

Fruit Cup—
Calcium hypochlorite (germicide wash)
Sodium chloride (prevent browning)
Sodium hydroxide (peeling agent)
Calcium hydroxide (firming agent)
Sodium metasilicate (peeling agent for peaches)
Sorbic acid (fungistat)
Sulfur dioxide (preservative)
FD&C red #3 (coloring for cherries)

Soup— Butylated hydroxyanisole (anti-oxidant)
Dimethyl polysiloxane (anti-foaming agent)
Sodium phosphate dibasic (emulsion for tomato soup)
Citric acid (dispersant in soup base)

Sandwich with Meat and Processed Cheese—
Sodium diacetate (mold inhibitor)
Mono-glyceride (emulsifier)
Potassium bromate (maturing agent)
Aluminum phosphate (improver)
Calcium phosphate monobasic (dough conditioner)
Chloramine T (flour bleach)
Aluminum potassium sulfate (acid-baking powder ingredient)
Ascorbate (anti-oxidant)
Sodium or potassium nitrate (color fixative)

Sodium chloride (preservative)
Guar Gum (binder)
Hydrogen peroxide (bleach)
FD&C Yellow #3 (coloring)
Nordihydroguaiaretic acid (anti-oxidant)
Alkanate (dye)
Methylviolet (marking ink)
Asafoetide (onion flavoring)
Sodium phosphate (buffer)
Magnesium carbonate (drying agent)
Calcium propionate (preservative)
Calcium citrate (plasticiser)
Sodium citrate (emulsifier)
Sodium alginate (stabilizer)
Chloramine T (deodorant)
Acetic acid (acid)
Pyroligneous acid (smoke flavor)

Fruit Pie—
Sodium diacetate (mold inhibitor)
Sorbic Acid (fungistat)
Butylated hydroxyanisole (anti-oxidant)
Sodium sulfite (anti-browning)
Mono-and-di-glycerides (emulsifier)
Agar-agar (thickening agent)
Calcium carbonate (neutralizer)
Aluminum ammonium sulfate (acid)
FD&C red #3 (cherry coloring)
Calcium chloride (apple pie mix firming agent)

Ice Cream—
Mono-and-di-glycerides (emulsifier)
Sodium citrate (buffer)
Amylacetate (banana flavoring)
Vanilldene Kectone (imitation vanilla flavoring)
Hydrogen peroxide (bactericide)

Bon Appétit!

Index